A Preface To Democratic Theory

BY *Robert A. Dahl*

THE UNIVERSITY OF CHICAGO PRESS

CHICAGO AND LONDON

CHARLES R. WALGREEN FOUNDATION LECTURES

The University of Chicago Press, Chicago 60637
The University of Chicago Press, Ltd., London

92 91 90   21 20 19 18

ISBN: 0–226–13425–3 (clothbound); 0–226–13426–1 (paperbound)
Library of Congress Catalog Card Number: 56–6642

Foreword

In presenting Professor Robert Dahl's *A Preface to Democratic Theory*, the Walgreen Foundation feels that it is adding another important volume to the growing number of works on the basic ideas of democracy. The Foundation has already presented works on democracy from the point of view of the philosopher and the moralist. In the field of political theory, however, many political theorists have been testing democratic ideas empirically. The Foundation welcomes Professor Dahl's work as representative of the empirical school. His contribution to the field of theory will undoubtedly be recognized by social scientists, no matter what school of thought they belong to.

JEROME G. KERWIN, *Chairman*
Charles R. Walgreen Foundation for
the Study of American Institutions

TO MARY

TABLE OF Contents

List of Illustrations vi

Introduction 1

1. *Madisonian Democracy* 4

2. *Populistic Democracy* 34

3. *Polyarchal Democracy* 63

4. *Equality, Diversity, and Intensity* 90

5. *American Hybrid* 124

Index 152

LIST OF
Illustrations

1. *Three Possible States of Public Opinion concerning Alternative Y* 57

2. *Strong Consensus with Strong Preferences* 93

3. *Strong Consensus with Weak Preferences* 93

4. *Moderate Disagreement: Symmetrical* 94

5. *Moderate Disagreement: Asymmetrical* 94

6. *Preferences of Voters in the 1952 Presidential Election* 95

7. *Preferences of Voters in the 1952 Presidential Election* 96

8. *Severe Disagreement: Symmetrical* 98

9. *Severe Disagreement: Asymmetrical* 99

10. *Popular Votes and House Seats* 148

11. *Popular Votes and Senate Seats* 149

Introduction

I have called these essays *A Preface to Democratic Theory* because for the most part they raise questions that would need to be answered by a satisfactory theory of democratic politics. They do not attempt to suggest all the questions that need to be answered, or even all the important ones, but only some I have found interesting and, I hope, significant.

It is anomalous, perhaps, that after so many centuries of political speculation, democratic theory should continue to be—if I am right in my basic assumption—rather unsatisfactory, whether the theory be regarded as essentially ethical in character or essentially an attempt to describe the actual world.

One of the difficulties one must face at the outset is that there is no democratic theory—there are only democratic theories. This fact suggests that we had better proceed by considering some representative democratic theories in order to discover what kinds of problems they raise; such a procedure is followed in these essays, although I have made no effort to survey all or most of the traditional theories about democracy.

That there are so many different approaches to democratic theory is partly, although not wholly, a result of the fact that there are so many possible approaches to any social theory, and in dealing with democracy a good case can be made out for almost all of these possibilities. A list of some of the alternative ways by which one might attempt to develop a theory about democracy is quite intimidating. I list some of them simply to indicate the appalling range of possibilities:

1. We might try to construct a maximizing theory, one that takes some state of affairs (such as political equality) as a value or goal and asks: What conditions are necessary to attain the maximum achievement of this goal? Or, alternatively we might try to construct a descriptive theory, one that in effect states something like this: Here is a set of social organizations that have this and that characteristic in common. Now what conditions are necessary in order for social organizations like this to exist?

2. If we choose a maximizing theory, we might try to construct one that is essentially ethical, in the sense that it seeks to justify, explain, or rationalize the values or goals to be maximized. Or we might try to construct one that is ethically neutral, in the sense that the goals or values are taken as given, at least for the purposes of the theory.

3. If we choose to construct an ethically neutral theory, we might seek an axiomatic theory or one that asks in effect: What logical prerequisites can I deduce from the description of the goal itself? Or we might seek an empirical theory, one that asks in effect: By observing the real world in some sense, what can I discover as necessary conditions (in the real world) for the maximization of the postulated goal?

4. We might be satisfied with a non-operational theory or demand that it be operational. (By operational I mean that the key definitions in the theory specify a set of observations about the real world, or a set of operations to be made upon the observations, or both.)

5. We might be satisfied with a theory that does not require any measurement, or we could demand that some of the phenomena be measurable. (By measurement I mean, at a minimum, the establishment of an order among the phenomena, so that A can be said to be greater than, equal to, or less than B, or some equivalent logical relation.)

6. We might construct a theory that lays down only constitutional prerequisites, or we could try to build one that includes the necessary social and psychological conditions.

I hope no one will be frightened off by this rather formidable set of alternatives, for I have no intention of subjecting the reader to a critique of each. Instead I shall take up a few representative types of democratic theory, beginning with one that is familiar to Americans: Madisonian theory. In the course of examining each of these types I shall also consider a few of the advantages and shortcomings of the principal alternatives mentioned above.

I do not propose to define "democracy" rigorously, for each of the chapters is to some extent an essay in definition—although each is, I feel, considerably more than that. But at a minimum, it seems to me, democratic theory is concerned with processes by which ordinary citizens exert a relatively high degree of control over leaders; this is a minimal definition that can be easily translated into a variety of more or less equivalent statements, should the reader not care for the particular language I choose to use.

Certain details that I find interesting and believe to be important, but which would mar the development of the argument for the reader concerned with the key points, I have put in the footnotes or in appendixes. In clarifying the argument to my own satisfaction, I found symbolization helpful, and because others may also find it helpful, I have included some of this material in the footnotes or appendixes. Like the other footnotes and appendixes these too may be ignored by the reader without significant loss to his grasp of the main argument.

I wish to express my deep appreciation to the Charles R. Walgreen Foundation for the Study of American Institutions for inducing me to prepare these chapters which were originally presented as Walgreen Lectures. I wish also to note here my debt to C. E. Lindblom, who not only read the manuscript in draft but gave me the benefit of many detailed criticisms and suggestions, all of which I benefited from, most of which I have tried to meet, and some of which I have rejected only at my great peril. Finally, I wish to record my thanks to Mrs. Suzanne Kernan, who did the typing and the seemingly endless retyping with skill and unlimited patience.

CHAPTER 1

Madisonian
Democracy

I

Democracy, it is frequently said, rests upon compromise. But democratic theory itself is full of compromises—compromises of clashing and antagonistic principles. What is a virtue in social life, however, is not necessarily a virtue in social theory.

What I am going to call the "Madisonian" theory of democracy is an effort to bring off a compromise between the power of majorities and the power of minorities, between the political equality of all adult citizens on the one side, and the desire to limit their sovereignty on the other. As a political system the compromise, except for one important interlude, has proved to be durable. What is more, Americans seem to like it. As a political theory, however, the compromise delicately papers over a number of cracks without quite concealing them. It is no accident that preoccupation with the rights and wrongs of majority rule has run like a red thread through American political thought since 1789. For if most Americans seem to have accepted the legitimacy of the Madisonian political system, criticism of its rather shaky rationale never quite dies down; and as a consequence, no doubt, the Madisonian theses must themselves be constantly reiterated or even, as with Calhoun, enlarged upon.

It would be misleading to ascribe all the propositions that follow directly to James Madison himself. For though Madison articulated most of the basic elements of the theory, before and at the Constitutional Convention and later in certain of the "Federalist Papers," his relation to the propositions that follow must be qualified in three ways.

First, despite dissents of varying sorts, much of what he set forth or implied was widely shared by other political leaders of his time. Madison, however, had the rare gift—doubly rare among political leaders—of lucid, logical, and orderly exposition of his theoretical argument; perhaps in no other political writing by an American is there a more compactly logical, almost mathematical, piece of theory than in Madison's *The Federalist*, No. 10. Hence it is both convenient and intellectually rewarding to turn to Madison to discover a basic rationale for the American political system.

Second, even Madison did not always articulate his assumptions as to fact, definition, or value. I have therefore found it necessary from time to time to supply what seem to me these implied assumptions. This is a risky business, and in defense I can only say that in every instance I have sought to make his position as orderly and coherent as possible and not to weaken it. In brief, I rely on Madison where he seems to make his own case most logical, consistent, and explicit, but in all other cases I try to formulate a proposition that seems to me more logical, consistent, and explicit. It is a style of argument I am concerned with, not a perfect reproduction of Madison's words.

Third, it is a little unfair to treat Madison as a political theorist. He was writing and speaking for his time, not for the ages. He was up to his ears in politics, advising, persuading, softening the harsh word, playing down this difficulty and exaggerating that, engaging in debate, harsh controversy, polemics, and sly maneuver. He was a great man, intelligent, principled, successful; and he built well. To take his ideas apart and examine them piece by piece is, undoubtedly, a little unfair. As an admirer of Madison the man and statesman, I would be content to let Madison the theorist lie in peace—if it were not for the fact that he so profoundly shaped and shapes American thinking about democracy.

The central proposition of the Madisonian theory is partly implicit and partly explicit, namely:

Hypothesis 1: If unrestrained by external checks, any given individual or group of individuals will tyrannize over others.

This proposition in turn presupposes at least two implied definitions:

DEFINITION 1: An "external check" for an individual consists of the application of rewards and penalties, or the expectation that they will be applied, by some source other than the given individual himself.[1]

DEFINITION 2: "Tyranny" is every severe deprivation of a natural right.

Three comments need to be made about the definition of tyranny supplied here. First, it is not the same as Madison's explicit definition of tyranny in *The Federalist*, No. 47, where he states that "the accumulation of all powers, legislative, executive, and judiciary, in the same hands, whether of one, a few, or many, may justly be pronounced the very definition of tyranny."[2] It seems to me that Madison's explicit definition has been derived from Definition 2 by the insertion of an empirical premise, i.e., the accumulation of all powers in the same hands would lead to severe deprivations of natural rights and hence to tyranny. It seems reasonable, therefore, to reconstruct Madison's explicit argument into the following Madisonian reasoning:

Hypothesis 2: The accumulation of all powers, legislative, executive, and judiciary in the same hands implies the elimination of external checks (empirical generalization).

The elimination of external checks produces tyranny (from Hypothesis 1).

Therefore the accumulation of all powers in the same hands implies tyranny.

As it stands Madison's explicit definition is unnecessarily arbitrary and argumentative, and since it can be derived from a definition that is not only highly congenial to the whole cast of Madison's thought

1. Hypothesis 1 and Definition 1 are a paraphrase, but I think a reasonably accurate paraphrase, of numerous references in Madison's writings. My language may be more modern, but the ideas are, I think, expressed by Madison, e.g., in his "Observations" of April, 1787, in *The Complete Madison, His Basic Writings*, ed. Saul K. Padover (New York: Harper & Bros., 1953), pp. 27–29. Cf. also his letter to Jefferson, October 24, 1787, pp. 40–43.

2. *The Federalist*, ed. Edward Mead Earle ("The Modern Library" [New York: Random House, n.d.]), p. 313. For another analysis of Madison see Mark Ashin, "The Argument of Madison's 'Federalist' No. 10," *College English*, XV (October, 1953), 37–45.

but, as will be shown in a moment, helpful to the logic of his argument, I propose to adhere to Definition 2.

Second, the natural rights are not clearly specified. Among Madison's contemporaries as among his predecessors there was by no means a perfect agreement as to what "rights" are "natural rights." Such agreement as existed was on a high level of abstraction and left wide opportunities for disagreement in specific cases.[3] As will be seen, the absence of an agreed definition of natural rights is one of the central difficulties of the Madisonian theory.

Third, I have used the expression "severe deprivation" to cover an ambiguity in the thought of Madison and his contemporaries. How far could governments go in limiting natural rights without becoming tyrannical? Here again, neither Madison nor any other Madisonian, so far as I am aware, has provided wholly satisfactory criteria. However, Madison no doubt agreed with his contemporaries that, at a minimum, any curtailment of natural rights without one's "consent" was a sufficiently severe deprivation to constitute tyranny.[4] The ambiguity is so deep-seated, however, that I doubt whether any phrasing can patch it up.

As corollaries of Hypothesis 1 two additional hypotheses need to be distinguished:

Hypothesis 3: If unrestrained by external checks, a minority of individuals will tyrannize over a majority of individuals.

Hypothesis 4: If unrestrained by external checks, a majority of individuals will tyrannize over a minority of individuals.

Or as Hamilton put it more succinctly, "Give all power to the many, they will oppress the few. Give all power to the few, they will oppress the many."[5]

3. Clinton Rossiter has summarized the state of agreement on natural rights at the time of the Revolution in *Seedtime of the Republic* (New York: Harcourt, Brace & Co., 1953), chap. xiii.

4. *Ibid.*, p. 383. Rossiter describes the consensus on this point.

5. *The Debates in the Several State Conventions on the Adoption of the Federal Constitution as Recommended by the General Convention at Philadelphia, in 1787, Together with the Journal of Federal Convention,* etc., ed. Jonathan Elliot (2d ed.; Philadelphia: Lippincott, 1941), V, 203. Hereafter this will be referred to as *Elliot's Debates.*

Let us now turn to the proof of Hypothesis 1, and hence also of Hypotheses 3 and 4.

II

Clearly Hypothesis 1 is an empirical proposition. Its validity can therefore be tested only by experience. Madison's own methods of validating the hypothesis seem to be representative of the widespread American style of thought that in this book is called "Madisonian." Madison's first method of proof is to enumerate historical examples drawn, for example, from the history of Greece and Rome.[6] His second method of proof is to derive the hypothesis from certain psychological axioms that were widely accepted in his day—and perhaps are now. These axioms are Hobbesian in character and run something like this: Men are instruments of their desires. They pursue their desires to satiation if given the opportunity. One such desire is the desire for power over other individuals, for not only is power directly satisfying but it also has great instrumental value because a wide variety of satisfactions depend upon it. The flavor of these axioms is conveyed in remarks at the state and federal conventions from both supporters and opponents of the Constitution:

Lenoir, in the North Carolina debates: "We ought to consider the depravity of human nature, the predominant thirst of power which is in the breast of everyone, the temptations rulers may have, and the unlimited confidence placed in them by this system."[7]

Franklin, at the Federal Convention: "There are two passions which have a powerful influence on the affairs of men. These are ambition and avarice; the love of power and the love of money."[8]

Hamilton, at the Federal Convention: "Men love power."[9]

Mason, at the Federal Convention: "From the nature of man, we may be sure that those who have power in their hands . . . will always, when they can, . . . increase it."[10]

III

If Hypothesis 1 is accepted as validated by these two methods (or others), then Hypotheses 3 and 4, which are merely derived from

6. E.g., Madison's remarks at the Convention, *ibid.*, p. 162.

7. *Ibid.*, IV, 204.

8. *Ibid.*, V, 145.

9. *Ibid.*, V, 200.   10. *Ibid.*, V, 294.

Hypothesis 1, are also valid. Nevertheless, Hypothesis 4 seems to play a special role in Madisonian thought.[11]

Neither at the Constitutional Convention nor in the "Federalist Papers" is much anxiety displayed over the dangers arising from minority tyranny; by comparison, the danger of majority tyranny appears to be a source of acute fear. The "Federalist Papers," for example, reveal no deep-seated distrust of the executive branch, which was regarded by the authors (wrongly, as it turned out) as the strong point for the minority of wealth, status, and power.[12] By contrast, a central theme of Madison's is the threat from the legislature, supposedly the stronghold of the majority. Thus: "It is against the enterprising ambition of this department that the people ought to indulge all their jealousy and exhaust all their precautions."[13]

And it follows from Definition 2, as well as from Madison's own explicit definition of tyranny, that legislative or majority tyranny is not any less tyrannical than executive or minority tyranny. They are equally undesirable. Thus: "The founders of our republics . . . seem never to have recollected the danger from legislative usurpations which, by assembling all power in the same hands, must lead to the *same* tyranny as if threatened by executive usurpations."[14] Madison buttressed his position by calling upon Jefferson, who in his *Notes on Virginia* had said, "One hundred and seventy three despots would surely be as oppressive as one . . . an *elective despotism* was not the government we fought for."[15]

Both majorities and minorities, then, are weighed on the same scales. For the objective test of non-tyranny is not the size of the ruling group;

11. For example, see Padover, *op. cit.*, pp. 28, 37–38, 41, 45–47. But see also Madison's "comment" in 1833, *ibid.*, p. 49. In later years Madison seems to have had a more tender regard for the majority principle. Like most Americans, Madison seems never to have felt any logical contradiction in his position.

12. Hamilton appears to have written the relevant papers, Nos. 67–77; given his political views, he might be expected to deprecate the dangers of tyranny from this branch. Moreover, it must never be forgotten that the "Federalist Papers" were polemical and propagandistic writing, reflecting a highly partisan viewpoint.

13. *The Federalist*, No. 48, p. 323.

14. *Ibid.*, p. 322. (Italics added.)

15. *Ibid.*, p. 324.

it is whether the ruling group, whatever its size, imposes severe deprivations on the "natural rights" of citizens.

IV

So far, the propositions in the Madisonian system are definitional or empirical. With the admission of one more definition, it now becomes possible to state the goals to be used in guiding the choice among possible political systems.

What is needed at this point is a definition of "democracy." However, in Madison's day the term "democracy" was less common than in ours. To some extent it was associated with radical equalitarianism; it was also ambiguous because many writers had defined it to mean what we today would call "direct" democracy, i.e., non-representative democracy. The term "republic" was frequently used to refer to what we would be more inclined to call "representative" democracy.[16] It will do no harm, therefore, to adhere to Madison's own term "republic," which he defined as follows:

DEFINITION 3: A republic is a government which (*a*) derives all of its powers directly or indirectly from the great body of the people and (*b*) is administered by persons holding their office during pleasure, for a limited period, or during good behavior.[17]

It is now possible to state the central ethical goal of the Madisonian system, which can conveniently be called the Madisonian axiom:

The goal that ought to be attained, at least in the United States, is a nontyrannical republic.

This goal was taken as a postulate. Because it was not seriously questioned at the Constitutional Convention or elsewhere and has never been seriously questioned in this country since that time, the goal has pretty much remained an unexamined axiom.[18] Hence one cannot

16. On this question, however, see the comment of Elisha P. Douglas, *Rebels and Democrats* (Chapel Hill: University of North Carolina Press, 1955), p. viii.

17. *The Federalist*, No. 39. "It is *essential* to such a government that it is derived from the great body of society, not from an unconsiderable proportion, or a favored class of it. . . . It is *sufficient* for such a government that the persons administering it be appointed, either directly or indirectly, by the people; and that they hold their appointments by either of the tenures just specified. . . ."

18. Cf. Louis Hartz, "The Whig Tradition in America and Europe," *American Political Science Review*, XLVI (December, 1952), 989–1002.

state unequivocally the rationale that may lie behind this postulate. To Madison and many others, however, the axiom was probably deduced implicitly from a more basic ethical postulate with the assistance of an empirical premise, as follows: (1) Natural rights ought to be attained (axiom); (2) attainment of natural rights is non-tyranny (from Definition 2); (3) a republic is a necessary although not a sufficient condition for non-tyranny (empirical generalization). Q.E.D.— the Madisonian axiom.

Although the first two of these propositions were widely accepted, some well-known Federalists like Hamilton denied the validity of the third. Hamilton, who had a frank but by then unrealistic preference for monarchy, said in effect that a republic might be a possible but it was assuredly not a necessary condition for non-tyranny; among the possible conditions for non-tyranny he would have included a constitutional monarchy. Fortunately for the stability of the American political system, but unfortunately for political theory, Hamilton's challenge was treated as a gigantic irrelevancy.

V

After this short excursion into ethical theory, the remainder of the Madisonian system consists of predictive statements, definitions, and inferences derived from what has been given so far. For, given the Madisonian axiom, the question now becomes: What conditions are necessary for attaining the goal of a non-tyrannical republic?

Hypothesis 5: At least two conditions are necessary for the existence of a non-tyrannical republic:

First Condition: The accumulation of all powers, legislative, executive, and judiciary, in the same hands, whether of one, a few, or many, and whether hereditary, self-appointed, or elective, must be avoided.[19]

Second Condition: Factions must be so controlled that they do not succeed in acting adversely to the rights of other citizens or to the permanent and aggregate interests of the community.[20]

VI

In attempting to prove that the first condition is an essential prerequisite of every non-tyrannical republic, the Madisonian system be-

19. *The Federalist,* No. 47, p. 313.
20. *The Federalist,* No. 10, pp. 57 ff.

comes so deeply ambiguous that it is difficult to know precisely how to do justice to the argument.

We are faced at the outset with two alternative possibilities. The first I rejected a moment ago as essentially trivial. For if we accept Madison's explicit definition of tyranny, and if we postulate that tyranny is to be avoided, then the first condition is necessary merely by definition: (1) Tyranny means the accumulation of all powers, etc. (definition). (2) Tyranny is undesirable (axiom). (3) Therefore the accumulation of all powers, etc., is undesirable. Yet to solve the problem by definition leaves open many major questions. For example, if one asks, "Why is tyranny as you define it undesirable?" the explicit Madisonian system proves no answer. For surely "the accumulation of all powers, legislative, executive, and judiciary, in the same hands" is not obviously or intuitively undesirable. The undesirability of such a state of affairs must then flow from certain predicted consequences. What are these consequences? To keep the Madisonian system intact, I took the liberty of specifying what these consequences must be, namely, "the severe deprivation of natural rights."[21]

Another possibility, therefore, is to accept Madison's implicit definition that tyranny is every severe deprivation of natural rights and to propose the empirical hypothesis that the accumulation of all powers, etc., will eliminate external checks (Hypothesis 2) and hence produce tyranny (by Hypothesis 1 and Definition 2).

Yet if we now attempt to retrieve the Madisonian system from a trivial argument by the addition of these implicit hypotheses and definitions, we are faced with a dilemma. For if by "power" we mean constitutionally prescribed authority, then the First Condition is demon-

21. Although the definition is not explicit in Madison's writings, so far as I can discover, it is clearly implied. For example, he argues in many places that in "a just and a free government . . . The rights both of property & of persons ought to be effectually guarded." But if there were universal suffrage and if the majority of citizens lacked property, then property rights might not be protected. Hence government must be so contrived as to prevent property rights from being infringed by majorities (Padover, *op. cit.*, pp. 37–38). Otherwise the government would not be "just & free." I have simply made "just & free" equivalent to "non-tyranny" and "tyranny" equivalent to non-"just & free," i.e., to deprivation of natural rights. If Madison's concept of "majority tyranny" has any other possible meaning than this, I have been unable to discover it.

strably false, for it is pretty clearly not necessary to every non-tyrannical republic, as an examination of parliamentary, but certainly non-tyrannical, democratic systems like that of Great Britain readily prove. Let us suppose, then, that by "power" we mean to describe a more realistic relationship, such as A's capacity for acting in such a manner as to control B's responses. Then it is plain that "legislative, executive, and judiciary" by no means comprise all the power relations or control processes in a society. For example, electoral processes make it possible for some individuals to control others; certainly they assist non-leaders in controlling leaders. Hence it is not obvious that the mere accumulation of legislative, executive, and judicial power must lead to tyranny, in the sense of severe deprivation of rights. Popular elections (and competing parties) might be sufficient to prevent such invasions of basic rights. That is, Madison's argument now seems to require proof of at least one additional hypothesis, namely:

Hypothesis 6: Frequent popular elections will not provide an external check sufficient to prevent tyranny.

For if this last hypothesis is false, and frequent popular elections will provide an external check sufficient to prevent tyranny, then Madison's argument about the need to keep the legislative, executive, and judicial powers constitutionally or otherwise separate in order to prevent tyranny is also patently false.

Now the explicit Madisonian system in effect tries to prove the validity of this hypothesis by assuming the validity of Hypothesis 2, that is, that the accumulation of all powers, legislative, executive, and judiciary, in the same hands implies the elimination of external checks. If we assume this hypothesis, then Hypothesis 6 on the inadequacy of popular elections must be true. But having proved Hypothesis 6 by assuming Hypothesis 2, we cannot now turn around and prove Hypothesis 2 by assuming the validity of Hypothesis 6.

The Federalist, No. 49,[22] to be sure, does attempt to prove that the

22. Although the authorship of this paper was once contested, it is now established that Madison, not Hamilton, was the author. (Irving Brant, *James Madison,* Vol. III: *Father of the Constitution, 1787–1800* [New York: Bobbs-Merrill Co., 1950], p. 184.)

check provided by electoral processes is inadequate to prevent all powers, legislative, executive, and judiciary, from accumulating in the same hands. Two observations can be made about this argument. First, even if the proposition is valid, it cannot establish the necessity of the First Condition except by the trivial definitional route rejected above. For, except by definition, it does not follow that the accumulation of "all powers, legislative, executive, and judiciary" leads to tyranny. Second, the specific arguments in support of the proposition in *The Federalist*, No. 49, seem to me patently invalid or highly inconclusive. They are (1) that frequent appeals would indicate defects in government and so weaken the veneration necessary to stability; (2) that public tranquillity would be dangerously disturbed by interesting public passions too strongly; (3) that being few in number, members of the executive and judiciary can be known only to a small part of the electorate; the judiciary are far removed, the executive are objects of jealousy and unpopularity. By contrast, members of the legislature dwell among the people and have connections of blood and friendship. Hence the contest for power would be an unequal one in which the legislature would swallow up the others.[23]

I am afraid, then, that the validity of the First Condition is not established.

Yet the necessity for this condition for a non-tyrannical republic is an article of faith in the American political credo. From it Madison, and successors who out-Madisoned Madison, have deduced the necessity for the whole complicated network of constitutional checks and balances: the separate constituencies for electing President, senators, and representatives; the presidential veto power; a bicameral Congress; presidential control over appointments, senatorial confirmation; and, in part, federalism. Over the years still other checks and balances within the political system have developed and have been

23. Madison also appends an argument more common among antidemocrats, namely, that issues in popular elections would not be decided on "the true merits of the question" but on a partisan basis. Unlike the first three, which seem to me plainly false, this one is merely meaningless—at least without a very considerable philosophical and empirical inquiry not attempted by Madison. Cf. *The Federalist*, No. 49, pp. 327–32.

rationalized by the same arguments: judicial review, decentralized political parties, the Senate filibuster, senatorial "courtesy," the power of committee chairmen, and indeed almost every organizational technique that promises to provide an additional external check on any identifiable group of political leaders.

VII

Let us now turn to the Second Condition: Factions must be so controlled that they do not succeed in acting adversely to the rights of other citizens or to the permanent and aggregate interests of the community.

How is this state of affairs to be attained? In answering this question, Madison produced one of the most lucid and compact sets of political propositions ever set forth by an American: the now familiar argument of *The Federalist*, No. 10.[24] I shall here attempt no more than to set forth the bare skeleton of his argument.

Obviously a definition is needed at the outset:

DEFINITION 4: A faction is "a number of citizens, whether amounting to a majority or a minority of the whole, who are united and actuated by some common impulse of passion, or of interest, adverse to the rights of other citizens, or to the permanent and aggregate interests of the community."[25]

Given this definition, it is easy to show from Hypothesis 1 that a faction will produce tyranny if unrestrained by external checks. Thus the Second Condition is proved to be necessary.

How, then, can factions be controlled? In brief, Madison argues with elegant rigor and economy that the latent causes of faction are sown in the nature of man: they stem from differences of opinion based on the fallibility of man's reason, from attachments to different leaders, and from differences in property, that are in turn a result of "the diversity in the faculties of men." If people cannot be made alike, the causes of faction could be controlled only by destroying liberty—a solution obviously barred to anyone seeking a non-tyrannical republic.

24. This represents a refinement of ideas Madison had already expounded at the Convention and earlier. Cf., for example, *Elliot's Debates*, V, 242–43.

25. *The Federalist*, No. 10, p. 54.

Hence it follows that factions cannot be controlled by eliminating their causes. In this fashion Madison proves the validity of

Hypothesis 7: If factions are to be controlled and tyranny is to be avoided, this must be attained by controlling the effects of faction.

Can the effects of faction be controlled so as to avoid tyranny? Yes, Madison tells us, provided two further conditions are present:

Hypothesis 8: If a faction consists of less than a majority, it can be controlled by the operation of "the republican principle" of voting in the legislative body, i.e., the majority can vote down the minority.

Hypothesis 9: The development of majority faction can be limited if the electorate is numerous, extended, and diverse in interests.

The validity of Hypothesis 8 must have seemed self-evident to Madison, for he made no effort to prove it. Yet it is an assumption of crucial importance to the Madisonian system; for if it can be shown that the operation of the "republican principle" will not in all cases prevent severe deprivations from being inflicted on the majority by the minority, then the Madisonian system will not produce a non-tyrannical republic. We shall return to this point.

Hypothesis 9 is proved by an argument that contains a number of exceedingly doubtful statements and some that, if true, raise serious questions as to the validity of other basic hypotheses in the Madisonian system. Madison argues that there are only two possible ways of controlling the effects of a majority faction. First, the existence of the same passion or interest in a majority at the same time must be prevented. But because in this case no majority faction would exist, Madison seems to have reversed his earlier argument that the causes of faction cannot be controlled. Second, even though a majority faction exists, its members must be made incapable of acting together effectually.

Both ways of controlling the effects of a majority faction, Madison argues, are provided by a large republic. There ensues an extremely dubious and probably false set of propositions purporting to show that representation in a large republic will provide "better" politicians and reduce the probability of success of "the vicious arts by which elections are too often carried." Then Madison states a final and exceptionally important proposition: "Extend the sphere, and you take in a greater variety of parties and interests; you will make it less probable that a majority of the whole will have a common motive to invade the rights of other citizens; or if such common motive exists, it will be more difficult . . . to act in unison."[26] Let us then paraphrase Madison:

Hypothesis 10: To the extent that the electorate is numerous, extended, and diverse in interests, a majority faction is less likely to exist, and if it does exist, it is less likely to act as a unity.

VIII

In the course of attempting to give meaning to the First Condition, it has already been necessary to examine its validity. Let us now turn to a brief appraisal of the validity of some of the other hypotheses and the utility of some of the definitions in the deliberately formalized Madisonian style of thought I have set forth so far.

The first hypothesis, it will be recalled, is implicit rather than explicit in the Madisonian argument, and it was formulated as follows:

Hypothesis 1: If unrestrained by external checks, any given individual or group of individuals will tyrannize over others.

DEFINITION 1: An external check for any individual consists of the application of rewards and penalties, or the expectation that they will be applied, by some source other than the given individual himself.

Inter alia, the first hypothesis implies:

1. That control over others by means of governmental processes is a highly valued goal, i.e., such control is believed to be either directly or indirectly rewarding to those who exercise it.

2. That it is impossible by social training to create through conscience a self-restraint sufficient to inhibit impulses to tyranny among political leaders. Madison in fact says as much: "Conscience—the only remaining tie—is known to be inadequate in individuals; in large numbers, little is to be expected from it."[27]

3. That the range of sympathetic identification of one individual with another is too narrow to eliminate impulses to tyranny.

Many political theorists prior to Madison placed heavy emphasis on the role of social indoctrination and habituation in creating attitudes,

26. *The Federalist,* No. 10, p. 61. Cf. also the last paragraph of *The Federalist,* No. 51, pp. 339 ff.

27. *Elliot's Debates,* V, 162.

habits, and even personality types requisite to a given type of political system. Machiavelli, who on the whole was not a soft-headed observer of human behavior, evidently believed that the basic check to tyranny was not so much a set of legal formulas about the prescribed distribution of certain controls—i.e., a formal constitution—as a network of habits and attitudes inculcated in the society. Surely this view is more in keeping with modern concepts of behavior than the one implicit in the Madisonian system. A contemporary social scientist would be inclined to assume that the prevailing type of family relationship, for example, would be at least as important a determinant of political behavior as the constitutionally prescribed system of governmental controls. Family structure, belief systems, myths, heroes, legitimate types of behavior in primary groups, prevailing or modal personality types, these and other similar factors would be crucial in determining the probable responses of leaders and non-leaders and hence the probability of tyranny or non-tyranny. Although scientific inquiry into this area has barely begun, it is clear that some personality types or predispositions are much more likely than others to lead to favorable or unfavorable attitudes toward authoritarian leaders. In the United States these predispositions may be related to such factors as class, education, and age.[28]

In other words, present evidence suggests that "internal checks"—the conscience (super-ego), attitudes, and basic predispositions—are crucial in determining whether any given individual will seek to tyrannize over others; that these internal checks vary from individual to individual, from social group to social group, and from time to time; and that the probability of tyranny emerging in a society is a function of the extent to which various types of internalized responses are present among members of that society.

Yet we should make Madison and his present-day followers seem

28. Morris Janowitz and Dwaine Marvick, "Authoritarianism and Political Behavior," *Public Opinion Quarterly*, XVII (summer, 1953), 185; also T. W. Adorno *et al., The Authoritarian Personality* (New York: Harper & Bros., 1950). I am indebted to my colleague, Professor Robert Lane, for calling my attention to the fact that if socioeconomic class is held constant, the other correlates do not appear to be statistically significant. Cf. his "Political Personality and Electoral Choice," *American Political Science Review*, XLIX (March, 1955), 173–90.

fools if we were to assume that they were oblivious to these or similar facts. Long before modern inquiry on authoritarian and democratic personality types, Jefferson, for example, insisted on the importance of a predominantly agricultural milieu for creating the kinds of behavior necessary to the operation of a democracy. Pre-Revolutionary writers had insisted upon moral virtue among citizens as a necessary condition for republican government. Virtue in the citizenry, they felt, in turn required "hortatory religion, sound education, honest government, and a simple economy."[29] In his explicit argument, however, Madison seems to have ignored or played down what must have been a common assumption of his time; no doubt here, as in many other points of the argument, we are confronted by a position oversimplified for purposes of debate and controversy. (Madison had more important tasks at hand than to satisfy the logic of critics a century and a half later.) Thus we might try to save one of Madison's basic implicit hypotheses by casting it in probability terms:

Hypothesis 1': The probability that any given individual or group will tyrannize over others if unrestrained by external checks is sufficiently high so that if tyranny is to be avoided over a long period, the constitutionally prescribed machinery of any government must maintain some external checks on all officials.

That is, it seems reasonable to propose that even if internal checks might frequently inhibit impulses to tyranny, they may not always do so with all individuals likely to be in a position to tyrannize. Hence, if tyranny is to be avoided, external checks are required. And these external checks must be constitutionally prescribed.

IX

Before we accept the reasonableness of the last sentence, however, let us examine some of the kinds of external checks that are used to control behavior. Let us assume that behavior is a product of one's conscious or unconscious expectations of rewards and penalties for one's socially modified drives.[30] What kinds of external checks does the Madisonian have in mind as restraints on tyranny?

29. Rossiter, *op. cit.*, pp. 429–32.

30. Note that when cast in psychological terms, the distinction between internal and external controls over behavior becomes somewhat hazy. Even in the case of

A mere demarcation on parchment of the constitutional limits of the several departments [he tells us] is not a sufficient guard against those encroachments which lead to a tyrannical concentration of all the powers of government in the same hands.[31]

To what expedient, then, shall we finally resort, for maintaining in practise the necessary partition of power among the several departments, as laid down in the Constitution? The only answer that can be given is, that as all these exterior provisions are found to be inadequate, the defect must be supplied, by so contriving the interior structure of the government as that its several constituent parts may, by their mutual relations, be the means of keeping each other in their proper places.

. . . The great security against a gradual concentration of the several powers in the same department, consists in giving to those who administer each department the necessary constitutional means and personal motives to resist encroachments of others. . . . Ambition must be made to counteract ambition. The interest of the man must be connected with the constitutional rights of the places.[32]

Now the more we examine these passages, the more they seem to dissolve before our eyes like the Cheshire cat. Why is the separation of powers necessary to prevent tyranny? Because it provides an external check on the tyrannical impulses of officials. Why does it provide an external check? Because it guarantees that the ambitions of individuals in one department will counteract those in another. Why will these countervailing ambitions be effective? Presumably because individuals in one department can invoke the threat of rewards and penalties against tyrannical individuals in another department. What then are these rewards and penalties?

Here we come to the core of the question. Presumably they are not such things as loss of status, respect, prestige, and friendship— unless it be argued that the mere fact of constitutional prescription will

internal control by conscience, the cue that evokes the expectation of punishing guilt feelings or "an attack of conscience" may well be an external object or action. Further, even when rewards and penalties are manipulated by a source outside the given individual, e.g., in the case of income or respect, it is the inner expectation or actual sensation of gratification or deprivation that is controlling. Here again, Madisonian theory probably cannot be satisfactorily converted into modern political science without such extensive surgery that the result would not be consistent with the style of thought we have here labeled "Madisonian."

31. *The Federalist*, No. 48, p. 326.

32. *The Federalist*, No. 51, pp. 335–37.

itself convey legitimacy and illegitimacy to certain actions; that officials who undertake illegitimate actions will suffer loss of status, respect, prestige, and friendship; and that these penalties are sufficient to prevent tyranny. But certainly this is not Madison's argument. Nor can the rewards and penalties depend on money, for the Constitution was contrived to restrict this means of control, lest the legislature become all powerful.

Do the rewards and penalties then involve the threat of physical coercion? In this category might be impeachment and conviction, and use of the armed forces. But in this case, a republic must always be on the verge of violence and civil war; for if physical coercion is the central restraint on tyranny, and if tyranny is the basic danger the argument assumes it to be, then the threat of physical coercion and therefore of violence can never be far removed from the operation of politics. Furthermore, if the main restraint is the threat of physical coercion, why would the leaders of a majority ever refrain from tyrannizing over a minority—at least if the majority were thought to be physically more powerful than the minority? Taking a more modern look at the way in which coercive control is distributed, why would a minority with control over the instruments of violence and coercion refrain from tyrannizing over a majority?

The fact is that in some nations powerful minorities have not refrained and tyranny has resulted; yet in other nations they have refrained. And whether or not powerful minorities or mass-based dictatorial leaders have refrained from establishing tyranny is clearly not related to the presence or absence of constitutional separation of powers. Many variables are involved in such a situation, but the constitutional separation of powers cannot be established as one of them.

Thus the Madisonian style of argument provides no satisfactory answer to the fundamental questions it raises. Madison evidently had in mind a basic concept, namely, that of reciprocal control among leaders. But in several ways, the Madisonian argument is inadequate:

1. It does not show, and I think cannot be used to show, that reciprocal control among leaders, sufficient to prevent tyranny, requires con-

stitutionally prescribed separation of powers, as in the American Constitution.

2. Either the significance of constitutional prescription as an external check is exaggerated or the argument misunderstands the psychological realities implied by the concept of a check on, or control over, behavior. And the inferences from either type of incorrect premise to propositions about political behavior or the requisites of a non-tyrannical democracy are false.

3. The Madisonian argument exaggerates the importance, in preventing tyranny, of specified checks to governmental officials by other specified governmental officials; it underestimates the importance of the inherent social checks and balances existing in every pluralistic society. Without these social checks and balances, it is doubtful that the intragovernmental checks on officials would in fact operate to prevent tyranny; with them, it is doubtful that all of the intragovernmental checks of the Madisonian system as it operates in the United States are necessary to prevent tyranny.

X

In the preceding discussion I have assumed that "tyranny" in the Madisonian system is a meaningful term. By assuming it to be meaningful, it has been possible to show that Hypothesis 1 leads to false conclusions. Now, however, we must ask whether the concept of "tyranny" implicit in the Madisonian system, and basic to the usual rationale of the American constitutional framework, has any operational meaning.

Tyranny, it will be recalled, was defined above as meaning every severe deprivation of a natural right. I have already explained why this definition seems to be required; indeed the idea of majority tyranny, against which the Madisonian system is erected, can only mean that a majority acting through regular processes of elections, legislation, and majority rule may nevertheless act in such a way as to deprive a minority of its natural rights.

Now I wish to avoid here a discussion of the concept of "natural right" and its utility in political theory, for this would take us very far afield into a voluminous and almost endless subject. Nevertheless, if I am right in thinking that by "tyranny" Madison meant to include "every severe deprivation of a natural right," then we cannot very well appraise the utility of this definition without considering the concept of natural right. I think, however, that we can get ourselves out of this dilemma in the following way.

We do not need to settle the question whether individuals have natural rights or, if they do, what these may be. All we need to know is whether anything roughly equivalent to the definition of tyranny I have supplied (the only alternative seemed to lead us into an essentially trivial defense of Madison's key First Condition) provides a useful concept in Madison's system. If it does not, then the idea of tyranny, which of course is central to Madison's argument, will have to be left in a highly unsatisfactory state.

It is self-evident that the definition of tyranny would be entirely empty unless natural rights could somehow be defined. It can be shown, I think, that we must specify a process by which specific natural rights can be defined in the context of some political society. To specify this process creates some dilemmas for the Madisonian.

If a natural right were defined, rather absurdly, to mean the right of every individual to do what he wishes to do, then every form of government must be tyrannical; for every government restrains at least some individuals from doing what they wish to do. For example, in this sense every government tyrannizes over criminals, whether these are defined by our own government or that of the U.S.S.R. A non-tyrannical republic would therefore be impossible. So this meaning of tyranny must be excluded.

It follows that tyranny must be defined to mean that severe penalties are inflicted only on some kinds of behavior. How are these kinds of behavior, which it is tyrannical to restrain, to be specified in practice? One possibility is to restrain only those kinds of behavior that every individual (or every adult) in the community believes to be undesirable. But this would require unanimity for governmental actions and would thereby make government impossible. For example, under this rule, if one murderer were to deny that murder is undesirable, the community could not punish murder. The unanimity rule of the United Nations Security Council would be the rule of all republics. Clearly the Madisonian system does not demand this.

The typical political situation is one in which individuals in a group or a society disagree as to the desirability of penalizing or rewarding certain kinds of behavior. Governmental processes are then employed to adjudicate the dispute. But when individuals disagree, what rule is to be employed to determine whether the punishing of some specified act would or would not be tyrannical? One possibility is to permit the majority to decide. I will examine some of the problems associated with this rule in chapter 2. Yet since this operating rule is precisely what Madison meant to prevent, and moreover would make the concept of majority tyranny meaningless, we must reject it. The only remaining possibility, then, is that some specified group in the community, not defined as the majority, but not necessarily always in opposition to it, would be empowered to decide. But if Hypothesis 1 is correct, then any group in the community with such a power would use it to tyrannize over other individuals in the community. Hence, in practice, no one could have the power to decide this question. Hence this definition of tyranny seems to have no operational meaning in the context of political decision-making.[33] And, of course, it follows further that, if tyranny has no operational meaning, then majority tyranny has no operational meaning.

Lest it be said that I have first rejected Madison's definition of tyranny and then deliberately substituted a definition that leads to foolish consequences, and have thus only set up a straw man in order to demolish him, let me say in defense: first, that for the reasons already given, Madison's own definition is a trivial one; second, that the definition I have given is implicit in his system; and third, that no alternative definition consistent with and necessary to the argument of his system as a whole can, I believe, escape the difficulties involved in the definition I have supplied.

33. It might be said that each individual would decide himself, upon consulting his own value system, whether or not a given act was tyrannical. But this is merely a prescription for individual behavior and provides no rule for a collective decision.

XI

If we turn to Madison's explicit concept of faction, we find that it suffers from the same difficulties as the implicit concept of tyranny. It would hardly be worth while to examine Madison's explicit concept of faction, however, if it were not for the fact that some such thought is implicit in many other attempts to defend the idea of constitutionally prescribed checks on "majorities."[34] The reader will recall Definition 4: A faction is "a number of citizens, whether amounting to a majority or a minority of the whole, who are united and actuated by some common impulse of passion, or of interest, adverse to the rights of other citizens, or to the permanent and aggregate interests of the community."

The difficulty with this definition of a faction is similar to the difficulty encountered with "tyranny." How can one use this concept? We can read it to mean that a faction is any group of citizens bent on invading the natural rights of others. Because such an action is tyrannical (by definition, even if the definition is a troublesome one), then obviously factions must be restrained if a non-tyrannical republic is to exist. A republic that avoids tyranny must avoid tyranny.

The definition would cease to be redundant if it could help us in some way to distinguish a "number of citizens" who make up a "faction" from any other number of citizens. Unless we can make such a distinction, the important subsequent propositions that depend upon the distinction are meaningless. Do factions have recognizable stigmata?

It is easy to see that so long as we do not know either the "rights of other citizens" or the "permanent and aggregate interests of the community," we are helpless. In the face of this difficulty, one might suggest a different approach. Instead of asking for the definitional characteristics of a faction, we might try to imagine some political process by which factions could be designated as situations arose. Admittedly

34. The quotation marks reflect my belief that in the usual sense intended, majorities rarely, if ever, rule in any country or social organization at any time. Thus the fear of majority rule, as well as the advocacy of it, is founded upon a misconception of the probabilities permitted by political reality. For discussion of this point, see chap. 5.

this is not what Madison had in mind, but it may be helpful to pursue this path, since Madison himself has left us without a guide.

Now if everyone always agreed what specific actions were "adverse to the rights of other citizens, or to the permanent and aggregate interests of the community," then a faction could be specified by unanimity. But both of these criteria are highly ambiguous, and unanimity is most improbable. Nearly all governmental actions deprive some individuals of legal rights they had previously possessed, and nearly all political groups seek some kind of governmental action that will deprive some individuals of certain existing legal rights. Hence rights must be read to mean natural rights; but as we have shown, consensus is lacking on what kinds of behavior are included in natural rights, particularly in concrete instances. As to the "permanent and aggregate interests of the community," so far as I am aware no political group has ever admitted to being hostile to these.

But if unanimity is not required, then something less than unanimity be sufficient. Yet if a majority is permitted to decide what constitutes a faction, and to invoke the appropriate machinery against that faction, then in practice a majority would never be a faction. For example, in practice a legislative majority might be permitted to determine what policies are "adverse to the rights of other citizens, or to the permanent and aggregate interests of the community." It might then simply vote down any such proposed policy. But it is highly improbable that a majority in favor of a given policy would ever decide that its own policy was factional and thereupon vote it down. Indeed, such an action is entirely inconceivable within the Madisonian framework of political behavior, and it is hardly conceivable within any other. Hence if majority factions are held to be a genuine danger, as Madison and his contemporary followers insist, then the determination of the meaning of faction by the majority itself would make the concept useless within the Madisonian context.

If determination by unanimity and by majority vote are both ruled out, it follows that the only remaining alternative is determination by the decision of some minority. But the preceding argument against resting this power in a majority certainly applies to any minority; if

Hypothesis 1 is correct, then we should expect any minority with this power at best to employ it in its own favor and at worst to tyrannize over other minorities and any majority.

XII

It is not part of my purpose to examine every detailed aspect of the Madisonian viewpoint. Yet one more major point is worth considering.

Protection against factions and therefore against tyranny, it will be recalled, requires two conditions:

Hypothesis 8: If a faction consists of less than a majority, it can be controlled by the operation of "the republican principle" of voting in the legislative body, i.e., the majority can vote down the minority.

Hypothesis 9: The development of majority faction can be limited if the electorate is numerous, extended, and diverse in interests.

Because, as we have seen, the terms "factions" and "tyranny" have been given no specific meaning, as they stand these two hypotheses also have no specific meaning, i.e., no conceivable way exists by which we can test their validity. Hence they remain mere untestable assertions.

To dispatch them in this ruthless way would no doubt leave many readers as unsatisfied as it does me. For one cannot escape the feeling that these propositions are at least worthy of examination if they could somehow be recast so as to overcome the deficiencies of their key terms. What repairs can we make in these concepts in order to test Hypotheses 8 and 9, so far as they may be tested at all?

It might be thought that the difficulties could be escaped in the following way. Let us first postulate that deprivations of freedom should be minimized. Let us then define the "freedom" of an individual as the opportunity to achieve his goals without external restraints. We now propose the following rule: the process of governmental policy-making will be so constructed that every group of a "significant" size will have an opportunity to veto threatened deprivations of its freedom. In this way no group's freedom is likely to be curtailed, except through ignorance, guile, etc.

This formulation involves several difficulties, one of the most important of which is that probably very few people would regard it as reasonable to concede the veto to every group of significant size. Most people, for example, would not grant the veto to criminals even if criminals were a group of significant size. If exceptions must be made, some individuals must make the exceptions; and we then find ourselves running through the maze of dilemmas already witnessed in the preceding discussions of tyranny and faction.

Let us suppose, however, that this problem could somehow be solved and made consistent with Madisonian principles, and that some but not all minorities could be given an effective veto. (As will be seen in chapter 5, something like this actually seems to operate in the American political system.) We may now test the validity of Hypothesis 8. According to this hypothesis, a minority bent on imposing severe deprivations on some majority could simply be voted down in the legislative body. Hence no minority could ever curtail the freedom of a majority through governmental action.

If we leave to one side the difficulties arising out of the majority's customary political passivity about issues at the policy-making stage, then Hypothesis 8 is valid provided that it is narrowly interpreted. By narrowly interpreted, I mean the hypothesis must specify that the majority needs to be larger than the minority by only one person. If a qualified majority is required to pass legislation—that is, a majority greater than the minority by more than one, as when a two-thirds or a three-fourths majority is necessary—then it can easily be shown that Hypothesis 8 will meet threats to the majority only if these threats arise from proposed government action. For if more than a bare majority is required to enact policy, then a minority of the appropriate size can veto any policy it dislikes. If the freedom of some majority is already curtailed in a such way that only positive governmental action will eliminate that deprivation, and if a minority with a veto dislikes the measures proposed to increase majority freedom, then by exercising its veto a minority can maintain deprivations of the freedom of a majority and hence can tyrannize over it.[35]

35. Although Madison seems never to have distinguished this situation clearly, I think he understood it and assumed the narrower meaning of Hypothesis 8. Thus in 1830 he opposed the nullification doctrine if it meant that "the decision of the state is to be presumed valid, and that it overrules the law of the United States,

Thus a majority might believe that child labor, low wages, bad housing, and the absence of effective trade-unions, social security, and slum clearance all represented severe deprivations of their freedom. In this case, the immediate deprivations would be inflicted by private individuals rather than governmental officials. Therefore if action by governmental officials is one necessary condition to eliminate child labor, low wages, and bad housing and to create effective trade-unions, social security, and decent housing; and, if, further, a minority, consisting, say, of employers (or officials responsive to or sympathetic with employers) can veto every government action intended to eliminate these privately imposed deprivations, then Hypothesis 8 is false. For in this case the "republican principle" would not be sufficient to protect a majority against the deprivations imposed by a minority.

XIII

Hypothesis 9 asserts that the effects of majority faction can be controlled if the electorate is numerous, extended, and diverse in interests. Here again, the absence of any definite meaning of the word faction is an obstacle to testing the prediction. Yet if we examine the arguments that Madison himself used to prove the validity of this hypothesis, it is clear that the hypothesis must be read to mean that the effectiveness of any majority whatsoever is severely limited if the electorate is numerous, extended, and diverse in interests. Whether or not the majority is factional is irrelevant to the operation of the restrictions imposed by the existence of a numerous, extended, and diverse electorate. Furthermore, so far as I am aware, no modern Madison has shown that the restraints on the effectiveness of majorities imposed by the facts of a pluralistic society operate only to curtail "bad" majorities and not "good" majorities; and I confess I see no way

---

unless overruled by three-fourths of the states." For, he argued, "to establish a positive and permanent rule giving such a power to such a minority, over such a majority, would overturn the first principle of free government. . . ." (Padover, *op. cit.*, pp. 157–58.) The concept of "minority veto" or "concurrent majorities" is not, strictly speaking, of Madison's creation. This view associated with the name of John C. Calhoun nevertheless seems to have become a fundamental element in the American ideology, and it is frequently defended in essentially Madisonian language.

by which such an ingenious proposition could be satisfactorily established.[36]

Hence the net effect of Hypothesis 9 seems to be this: because majorities are likely to be unstable and transitory in a large and pluralistic society, they are likely to be politically ineffective; and herein lies the basic protection against their exploitation of minorities. This conclusion is of course scarcely compatible with the preoccupation with majority tyranny that is the hallmark of the Madisonian style of thought.

XIV

The absence of specific meaning for terms like "majority tyranny" and "faction" coupled with the central importance of these concepts in the Madisonian style of thinking has led to a rather tortuous political theory that is explicable genetically rather than logically. Genetically the Madisonian ideology has served as a convenient rationalization for every minority that, out of fear of the possible deprivations of some majority, has demanded a political system providing it with an opportunity to veto such policies.[37]

At the formation of the Constitution, the Madisonian style of argument provided a satisfying, persuasive, and protective ideology for the minorities of wealth, status, and power who distrusted and feared their bitter enemies—the artisans and farmers of inferior wealth, status, and power, who they thought constituted the "popular majority." Today, however, it seems probable that for historically explicable reasons a preponderant number of politically active Americans believe themselves to be members, at least part of the time, of one or more minorities—minorities, moreover, whose goals might be threatened if the prescribed constitutional authority of majorities were legally unlimited. Hence, whatever its defects of logic, definition, and scientific utility, the Madisonian ideology is likely to remain the most prevalent and

36. Cf. chap. 4.

37. Calhoun's transparent defense of the southern slavocracy by his doctrine of concurrent majorities seems to me prone to all the weaknesses of the Madisonian system, which in many respects it parallels. But I have not tried to deal specifically with Calhoun's special variant on Madison. Cf. his *Disquisition on Government*, ed. R. K. Cralle (New York: Peter Smith, 1943), esp. pp. 28–38.

deeply rooted of all the styles of thought that might properly be labeled "American." One would be foolish indeed to suppose that an examination of its illogicality would significantly diminish its acceptance. Ideologies serve a variety of needs—psychological, socio-economic, political, propagandistic—that transcend the need of pedants for scientific cogency.

Nevertheless, as political science rather than as ideology the Madisonian system is clearly inadequate. In retrospect, the logical and empirical deficiencies of Madison's own thought seem to have arisen in large part from his inability to reconcile two different goals. On the one hand, Madison substantially accepted the idea that all the adult citizens of a republic must be assigned equal rights, including the right to determine the general direction of government policy. In this sense majority rule is "the republican principle." On the other hand, Madison wished to erect a political system that would guarantee the liberties of certain minorities whose advantages of status, power, and wealth would, he thought, probably not be tolerated indefinitely by a constitutionally untrammeled majority. Hence majorities had to be constitutionally inhibited. Madisonianism, historically and presently, is a compromise between these two conflicting goals. I think I have shown that the explicit and implicit terms of the compromise do not bear careful analysis. Perhaps it is foolish to expect them to.

In searching for a theory about democracy that will bear up under examination, two alternatives suggest themselves, each centered on achieving one of the two basic goals so dangerously allied by Madison's compromise. One possibility is to concentrate one's argument on Madison's worry that the majority will prevent the minority—or a particularly worthy minority—from achieving what it has a "right" to achieve, whether this be property, status, power, or the opportunity to save mankind. Following this line of thought, one would postulate that the goals of some particular set of individuals are inherently right or good, and the process of making decisions should insure the maximization of these goals. Ironically the worry about the dangers of majorities has been shared not only by aristocratic elites but also by political adventurers, fanatics, and totalitarians of all kinds, so that this style of thought takes many forms and finds advocates as different as Plato and Lenin. If we carry one aspect of Madison's argument to its logical limit, then, we can easily place him in the camp of the great antidemocratic theorists. But since Madison recoiled from pushing his premises to their limits, it would be unfair, foolish, and pointless to force his argument so far. Moreover, whatever one may think about the desirability of one or another of the political systems proposed by these theorists, it seems to me that unless we wish to eliminate some very useful distinctions among political systems, we cannot regard these systems, centered on the goal of avoiding majority control, as democratic. Madison, it seems to me, goes about as far as it is possible to go while still remaining within the rubric of democracy. Because of this, I do not propose to explore this alternative development out of Madison's argument.

The other alternative is to lay down political equality as an end to be maximized, that is,to postulate that the goals of every adult citizen of a republic are to be accorded equal value in determining government policies. If this were our objective, what basic conditions should exist for making government decisions? This is the alternative to which we now turn.

APPENDIX TO CHAPTER 1

Summary of the Madisonian argument

I. The basic definitions:

DEFINITION 1: An "external check" for any individual consists of the application of rewards and penalties, or the expectation that they will be applied, by some source other than the given individual himself.

DEFINITION 2: "Tyranny" is every severe deprivation of a natural right.

DEFINITION 3: A republic is a government which (*a*) derives all of its powers directly or indirectly from the great body of the people, and (*b*) is administered by persons holding their office during pleasure, for a limited period, or during good behavior.

DEFINITION 4: A faction is "a number of citizens, whether amounting to a majority or a minority of the whole, who are united and actuated by some common impulse of passion, or of interest, adverse to the rights of other citizens, or to the permanent and aggregate interests of the community."

II. The basic axiom: The goal that ought to be attained, at least in the United States, is a non-tyrannical republic.

III. The argument:

Hypothesis 1: If unrestrained by external checks, any given individual or group of individuals will tyrannize over others.

Hypothesis 2: The accumulation of all powers, legislative, executive, and judiciary, in the same hands implies the elimination of external checks.

Hypothesis 3: If unrestrained by external checks, a minority of individuals will tyrannize over a majority of individuals.

Hypothesis 4: If unrestrained by external checks, a majority of individuals will tyrannize over a minority of individuals.

Hypothesis 5: At least two conditions are necessary for the existence of a non-tyrannical republic:

First Condition: The accumulation of all powers, legislative, executive, and judiciary, in the same hands, whether of one, a few, or many, and whether hereditary, self-appointed, or elective, must be avoided.

Second Condition: Factions must be so controlled that they do not succeed in acting adversely to the rights of other citizens or to the permanent and aggregate interests of the community.

Hypothesis 6: Frequent popular elections will not provide an external check sufficient to prevent tyranny.

Hypothesis 7: If factions are to be controlled and tyranny is to be avoided, this must be attained by controlling the effects of faction.

Hypothesis 8: If a faction consists of less than a majority, it can be controlled by the operation of "the republican principle."

Hypothesis 9: The development of majority factions can be limited if the electorate is numerous, extended, and diverse in interests.

Hypothesis 10: To the extent that the electorate is numerous, extended, and diverse in interests, a majority faction is less likely to exist, and if it does exist, it is less likely to act as a unity.

CHAPTER 2

Populistic Democracy[1]

I

Madison spoke of majority decisions as "the republican principle." This was, as we have shown, one part of his great compromise. Running through the whole history of democratic theories is the identification of "democracy" with political equality, popular sovereignty, and rule by majorities. Here, for instance, is Aristotle in the *Politics:*

> The most pure democracy is that which is so called principally from the equality which prevails in it: for this is what the law in that state directs; that the poor shall be in no greater subjection than the rich; nor that the supreme power shall be lodged with either of these, but that both shall share it. For if liberty and equality, as some persons suppose, are chiefly to be found in a democracy, it must be so by every department of government being alike open to all; but as the people are in the majority, and what they vote is law, it follows that such a state must be a democracy.

And numerous others have written in the same vein. For example:

> For when any number of men have, by the consent of every individual, made a community, they have thereby made that community one body, with a power to act as one body, which is only by the will and determination of the majority.
>
> The majority having . . . upon men's first uniting into society, the whole power of the community naturally in them, may employ all that power in making laws for the community from time to time . . . [Locke, *Second Treatise on Civil Government*].

1. The term "populistic democracy" was suggested to me by Edward Shils, in a paper "Populism and the Rule of Law," read at the University of Chicago Law School Conference on Jurisprudence and Politics, April, 1954.

There is but one law which, from its nature, needs unanimous consent. This is the social contract. . . .

Apart from this primitive contract, the vote of the majority always binds all the rest. . . .

This presupposes, indeed, that all the qualities of the general will still reside in the majority; when they cease to do so, whatever side a man may take, liberty is no longer possible [Rousseau, *Social Contract*].

All, too, will bear in mind this sacred principle, that although the will of the majority is in all cases to prevail, that will, to be rightful, must be reasonable [Jefferson, First Inaugural, March 4, 1801].

The first principle of republicanism is, that the lex-majoris partis is the fundamental law of every society of individuals of equal rights; to consider the will of the society enounced by the majority of a single vote, as sacred as if unanimous, is the first of all lessons in importance . . . [Jefferson, Letter to Baron von Humboldt, 1817].

Unanimity is impossible; the rule of a minority, as a permanent arrangement, is wholly inadmissible; so that, rejecting the majority principle, anarchy or despotism in some form is all that is left [Lincoln, First Inaugural, March 4, 1861].

The very essence of democratic government consists in the absolute sovereignty of the majority; for there is nothing in democratic states which is capable of resisting it [De Tocqueville, *Democracy in America*].

These prescriptions for, or descriptions of, the operation of democratic governments are clearly at odds with the Madisonian view. In practice, however, the attempt to identify democracy with the unlimited power of majorities has usually gone hand in hand with an attempt to include in the definition some concept of restraints on majorities. Locke left the argument sufficiently ambiguous to permit him to be regarded as the advocate both of unlimited majority government and of limited government. Jefferson was, after all, a "Madisonian" and supported the constitutional system erected during his absence. Lincoln found it useful in 1861 to insist on the divine right of majorities as an alternative both to secession and to Calhoun's "concurrent" majorities; but he did not essentially quarrel with the Madisonian constitutional system he sought to preserve. In referring to the absolute sovereignty of the majority, De Tocqueville was alluding to the United States: the very home of Madisonianism! The words quoted above are the opening sentence of a chapter entitled, "Unlimited Power of the Majority in the United States, and Its Consequences."

An examination of various statements of these incompatible positions suggests two conclusions. First, the assertion either of "absolute sovereignty of the majority" or of "absolute minority rights" encounters a number of quite formidable objections, and hence ideologues have served a variety of purposes in maintaining both positions at the price of logical consistency. In the United States the resulting logical confusion is almost incredible; but the long persistence of logical inconsistencies hints at the fulfilment of some deep-seated social need. In the United States this may be the minimization of severe conflicts.

Second, so far as I am aware, no one has ever advocated, and no one except its enemies has ever defined democracy to mean, that a majority would or should do anything it felt an impulse to do. Every advocate of democracy of whom I am aware, and every friendly definition of it, includes the idea of restraints on majorities. But one central issue is whether these restraints are, or should be, (1) primarily internalized restraints in the individual behavior system, such as the conscience and other products of social indoctrination, (2) primarily social checks and balances of several kinds, or (3) primarily prescribed constitutional checks. Among political systems to which the term "democracy" is commonly applied in the Western world, one important difference is between those which rely primarily on the first two checks, and those like the United States which also employ constitutional checks.

II

In what follows, I attempt to set forth an argument from which—to use De Tocqueville's phrase—the "absolute sovereignty of the majority" is sometimes derived. I shall then appraise this argument. Even more than in the case of the Madisonian argument, the task here is to make explicit certain assumptions and chains of reasoning that are ordinarily left implicit or tangential. So much is this so, that I shall not attribute the argument to any specified theorist at all.[2] Hence what fol-

2. Wolodymyr Starosolskyz, *Das Majoritätsprinzip* (Vienna and Leipzig, 1916), represents one of the few attempts at systematic analysis of the concepts involved in the principle of majority rule. It is in the grand style of German sociology of the

lows can be regarded as one way—and, I would argue, a way quite frequently implicit in democratic theories—of deriving the proposition that majorities should have unlimited sovereignty.

DEFINITION 1: An organization is democratic if and only if the process of arriving at governmental policy is compatible with the condition of popular sovereignty and the condition of political equality.

DEFINITION 2: The condition of popular sovereignty is satisfied if and only if it is the case that whenever policy choices are perceived to exist, the alternative selected and enforced as governmental policy is the alternative most preferred by the members.

DEFINITION 3: The condition of political equality is satisfied if and only if control over governmental decisions is so shared that, whenever policy alternatives are perceived to exist, in the choice of the alternative to be enforced as government policy, the preference of each member is assigned an equal value.

Proposition 1: The only rule compatible with decision-making in a populistic democracy is the majority principle.[3]

DEFINITION 4: THE RULE: The principle of majority rule prescribes that in choosing among alternatives, the alternative preferred by the greater num-

---

time, makes heavy use of dubious anthropological material, and is not very useful. Perhaps the single most succinct statement of the majority rule argument is in Henry Steele Commager, *Majority Rule and Minority Rights* (New York: Oxford University Press, 1943). The most exhaustive analysis is Wilmoore Kendall, *John Locke and the Doctrine of Majority Rule* (Urbana, 1941); cf. also the exchange between him and Herbert McClosky in *The Journal of Politics*, XI (November, 1949), 637–54, and XII (January, 1950), 694–713. I am grateful to him and Austin Ranney for their generosity in permitting me to examine in manuscript the first four chapters of their forthcoming book, *Democracy and the American Party System*, which also sets forth the theory concerning rule by majorities. Francis W. Coker has criticized the Kendall-Ranney position in "Some Present-Day Critics of Liberalism," *American Political Science Review*, XLVII (March, 1953), 1–27. Some of the elements in the populistic model and some of the weaknesses in the Madisonian model were set forth in my paper "Majority Rule and Civil Rights," delivered at the annual meeting of the American Political Science Association in 1948. I have also leaned heavily on the relevant chapters of a volume written jointly by Charles E. Lindblom and myself, *Politics, Economics, and Welfare* (New York: Harper & Bros., 1953). With his usual lucidity, George H. Sabine has examined the origins and characteristics of the democratic tradition that emphasizes "liberty" and the tradition that emphasizes "equality." Madisonian theory is an instance of the first, populistic theory is the essence of the second. See his "The Two Democratic Traditions," *The Philosophical Review*, LXI (October, 1952), 451. For the notational devices used in the footnotes and in the Appendix to this chapter, and for many insights into the argument, I am indebted to suggestions found in Kenneth Arrow, *Social Choice and Individual Values* (New York: John Wiley & Sons, 1951).

3. A proof of this proposition will be found in the Appendix to this chapter.

ber is selected. That is, given two or more alternatives x, y, etc., in order for x to be government policy it is a necessary and sufficient condition that the number who prefer x to any alternative is greater than the number who prefer any single alternative to x.

Proposition 2: Populistic democracy is desirable, at least for governmental decisions, as a final appeal when other specified processes have been exhausted, and among adult citizens (the condition of "the last say").

The Rule, as I shall call Definition 4 for the sake of convenience, may be thought of as a norm actually governing the behavior of individuals in a given system when governmental decisions are made. We do not have to decide whether it is or is not also a constitutional rule. All we need to specify is that whatever the constitutional rules may be, they must not lead to behavior incompatible with the Rule. Likewise we do not need to decide whether individuals agree to the Rule, or, if they do, what proportion agrees. Again, all we need to specify is that whatever the state of agreement may be, it must not produce behavior incompatible with the Rule. Thus what is asserted in Proposition 1 is that if the conditions of popular sovereignty and political equality are to be satisfied, then the individuals in the political system must behave in accordance with the Rule. By putting it in this way, I think we avoid a number of ticklish problems that would otherwise delay us from moving directly to the central issues in the argument.

III

Objections to this approach to democracy can be rather arbitrarily lumped into three groups, depending on whether they are technical, ethical, or empirical.

Of the technical objections, we shall discuss four. First, the argument has apparently assumed that each citizen does have a preference for one alternative. Yet in fact, it may be objected, many citizens might be and usually are indifferent as to the outcome. However, this is not really a substantial objection, for given the assumptions of Proposition 1, the indifferent citizen may properly be ignored and only those with preferences need be considered.[4] That is, the Proposition applies

4. If we designate by the symbol *NI* "the number of citizens who are indifferent as to the outcome in a choice between two alternatives," and if we designate the alternatives as "x" and "y," then we can write "the number of citizens indifferent

to individuals with preferences and not to individuals without preferences. Hence the fact that many citizens are indifferent as to the
alternatives does not affect the logic of the argument: to satisfy the
Rule, it is sufficient to know the number who prefer each alternative,
for to add the preferences of the indifferent would of course not influence the outcome.[5]

A second and correct technical objection is that the majority principle provides no solution for cases where each of the alternatives is
preferred (or voted for) by an equal number of citizens. An inspection
of Definition 4 reveals this to be so. It might be proposed that in all such
cases an appropriate interpretation of Proposition 1 would require
governmental indifference or deadlock. Certainly no other solution is
formally compatible with the Rule.[6]

Nonetheless, it is easy to be misled by the word "indifferent," for,
psychologically speaking, the members of the community and therefore
the community might be anything but indifferent. If deadlock occurs
in a choice beween two alternatives that are very highly ranked by the
respective partisans, then violence and civil war may well result. His-

---

as between alternatives x and y" simply as $NI(x, y)$. Likewise we can write
$NP(x, y)$ meaning "the number of citizens who prefer x to y." Now by definition
$NI = NI(x, y) = NI(y, x)$.
    Therefore

$$NP(x, y) \geq NP(y, x) \rightarrow NP(x, y) + NI \geq NP(y, x) + NI. \qquad (1)$$

(The connective symbols $\rightarrow$ and $\leftrightarrow$ will be used to mean "implies" and "A implies
B and conversely," respectively. They may also be read to mean "A is a sufficient
condition for B" and "A is a necessary and sufficient condition for B," respectively.)

5. Assuming that indifference does not merely reflect ignorance of the alternatives and their consequences. In the real world, political indifference (apathy) is in
fact inversely proportional to education and several other indices of knowledge.

6. Symbolically, the Rule may be stated as follows:

$$NP (x, y) > NP (y, x) \leftrightarrow x \, Pg \, y,$$

where $x \, Pg \, y$ means "x is preferred by government to y" or "x rather than y is chosen
as government policy." But obviously if $NP(x, y) = NP(y, x)$, then the Rule gives
no instructions for a solution; but it does tell us that no solution must provide for
x as the chosen policy, and also that no solution must provide for y, i.e., government
policy must be indifferent as between x and y. Or symbolically:

$$NP (x, y) = NP (y, x) \rightarrow x \, Ig \, y . \qquad (2)$$

torically this may have been the situation that actually developed in the United States during the years 1850–60, when a substantial number of individuals with preferences about slavery became polarized around the two mutually exclusive alternatives: extension of slavery into the territories *vs.* exclusion of slavery from the territories. The deadlock became intolerable, and it was only broken by Lincoln's election and the Civil War.

Hence, in any case where citizens are split into roughly equal groups, each preferring its own alternative and the rejection of the other group's alternative to such values as social peace, avoidance of violence, national cohesion, etc., no solution compatible with the Rule is possible. For in this case deadlock—the only formally compatible condition—will not be accepted, and one side will seek to impose its preferences on the other by any means at its disposal. Thus the majority principle would have to be set aside.

Now it may be said that the objection is founded upon a case which is so unlikely to occur as to make the objection trivial.[7] Nevertheless, the objection suggests several important conclusions. To begin with, the Rule presupposes the existence of certain empirical conditions (e.g., a high consensus on the Rule itself) that have not been specified; in the absence of these conditions, the Rule is irrelevant. And if one believed that the conditions were insufficiently present to make the Rule operable in the United States, for example, then it would be entirely consistent to argue that the goals of popular sovereignty and political equality, although strictly unattainable in the United States, might be most closely approximated there by some alternative other than the majority principle.

7. So far as I know, no one has made an investigation of the occurrence of tie votes in various sized bodies. The task would be gigantic, and I do not propose it. If we assume that every possible arrangement of preferences among two alternatives were equally likely, e.g., that among 10 individuals, divisions of 10 for and 0 against, 0 for and 10 against, and 5 for and 5 against are equally probable, then the probability of a 50–50 division on any given issue would be only $1/(N + 1)$, where N is the number of votes cast. But a 50–50 division is possible only if N is even; if we assume an equal chance that N will be even or odd, then the probability of a 50–50 division in general would be $1/2(N + 1)$. These assumptions are arbitrary; in the American Congress or the House of Commons one would expect divisions to cluster around 50–50 and close to unanimity.

Furthermore, in the real world, even in a constitutional system based upon the majority principle (as in France), deadlock or violence evidently do not require two groups of perfectly equal size.

Finally, if deadlock is the only solution compatible with the Rule under the conditions given, then the possibility is at least suggested that the closer a group approached to an equal division the less valid the majority principle becomes. It is a necessary inference from the definition of the majority principle that even if the majority exceeds the minority by one vote, the majority principle nevertheless applies. Yet the application of the majority principle in such an extreme case where the group is large and the difference very slight might strike one at worst as doctrinaire absurdity and at best as a mere matter of convenience.

A third technical objection to the Rule stems from the preceding one. As we have just shown, in cases of an equal division of preferences among citizens, the only solution compatible with the Rule is governmental deadlock. But in certain cases of an equal division of preferences, even this solution is self-contradictory. Suppose that x is existing policy, and y is an alternative to it requiring governmental action, e.g., x is a policy of non-interference by the federal government in lynching cases and y is legislation requiring the federal government to intervene. If the deadlock solution is followed, then no governmental action is taken; but if no governmental action is taken, then in fact x is government policy. Thus, by prescribing deadlock in cases of equal division of preferences (votes), one is in fact biasing the policy-making process in favor of all individuals who prefer policies requiring government inaction and against all individuals who prefer policies requiring government action. Yet if the deadlock solution is not followed the results would be equally arbitrary. Hence in such cases, the deadlock solution is self-contradictory, and no outcome can be shown to be compatible with Proposition 1 and the Rule.

Here again, the main practical conclusion is that the closer a group approaches to an equal division, the more any rule seems to be a mere matter of convenience, given the values underlying Proposition 1.

The third objection can be generalized to cover all cases where preferences (votes) are distributed among equal groups.[8] In all such cases, not only is the Rule irrelevant but no satisfactory rule compatible with the conditions of popular sovereignty and political equality can be adduced.[9]

8. This aspect of the third objection and also the fourth objection are drawn from E. J. Nansen, "Methods of Election," *Transactions and Proceedings of the Royal Society of Victoria*, XIX (1883), 197–240. Kenneth Arrow has called attention to the significance of the objection in his *Social Choice and Individual Values* (New York: John Wiley & Sons, 1951), p. 3.

9. Let us suppose three alternatives, x, y, and z, and the body of citizens divided into three equal groups as follows:

> Group A prefers x to y, and y to z, and x to z.
> Group B prefers y to z, and z to x, and y to x.
> Group C prefers z to x, and x to y, and z to y.

Since Group A and Group B both prefer y to z, and since together they comprise two-thirds of the citizens, it might be thought that y should be the choice. Yet Group A and Group C both prefer x to y, and hence it might be thought that x should be the choice. But Group B and Group C both prefer z to x. Thus each alternative is preferred by one combination of groups; and yet another combination of groups in each case prefers another alternative. Here no solution compatible with the conditions of popular sovereignty and political equality is possible. Because Arrow, *op. cit.*, assumes "transitivity of collective choice" as a criterion of rational social action, it is worth noting that under almost any theory of democratic politics, and certainly under the one in question here, the requirement of transitivity would be irrational in a great many types of collective choices. By "transitivity" we mean, on the analogy of inequalities in mathematics, that if an individual prefers x to y and y to z he must also prefer x to z—at least, if he is to behave rationally. But whatever the case may be with individual choices—and even here the requirement is somewhat tendentious—clearly it would lead to irrational results in a democracy to require transitivity in collective choices. For example, among 101 individuals assume that

> 1 individual prefers x to y, and y to z,
> 50 individuals prefer z to x, and x to y,
> 50 individuals prefer y to z, and z to x.

Then 51 prefer x to y, 51 prefer y to z. If we assume transitivity in collective choice, it would follow that a majority of at least 51 prefers x to z also. But in fact, 100 individuals prefer z to x. And the requirement of transitivity would produce the anomalous result that the preferences of the singular eccentric would be translated into public policy despite the fact that 100 individuals prefer the opposite policy. Arrow shows that if there are more than two alternatives, any method for making social decisions that insures transitivity in the decisions must necessarily be either dictated by one person or imposed against the preferences of every individual (pp. 51–59). The only restraint on individual choices assumed is that they are (1) "connected," i.e., no individual can prefer x to y and at the same time prefer y to x or be indifferent as between x and $y;$ and (2) "transitive," in the sense indicated above. However, given certain further restrictions on the possible orderings of indi-

The fourth objection is that even if a majority exists, in the sense that more citizens or legislators prefer one alternative to another, it may be impossible to find a voting method that satisfies the Rule and at the same time meets certain practical requirements. It would be tedious to demonstrate the difficulties of various voting methods, particularly since these have been thoroughly examined by others.[10] It is sufficient to say that whenever there are more than two alternatives at issue, each of the following methods of voting can produce a collective choice that violates the preferences of a majority:[11] the single-vote method, whereby each voter casts one vote designating his single most preferred choice; the single-vote method followed by a runoff of the highest choices; the double-vote method, whereby each voter votes for two alternatives, and the alternative with the highest number of votes is selected; and Borda's method, whereby each elector has three votes, two being given to one alternative and one to another.

The essential requirement of a system of voting that will satisfy the Rule is that voters, whether citizens, legislators, or committee members, must have an opportunity to vote for each alternative paired with another of the alternatives in a series of pairs sufficiently complete so that the alternative most preferred by a majority, if one such exists, will necessarily be selected. In some cases, this requires that a vote be cast on every pair of alternatives.[12]

---

vidual choices (they must be "single-peaked"), the method of majority rule will result in decisions that are transitive, and at the same time are neither imposed nor dictatorial (pp. 75–80). This brilliantly developed and quite startling argument has, unfortunately, so far been totally ignored by political scientists.

10. Especially by Nansen, *op. cit.*, whom the reader should consult for technical criticism of the single-vote method, the single vote with a runoff, the double-vote method, Borda's method, and for Nansen's own proposal. Cf. also Alfred de Grazia, "Mathematical Derivation of an Election System," *Isis*, Vol. XLIV (June, 1953), for a translation of and comment on Borda's "Memoir on Elections by Ballot," first published in 1781.

11. Voting by proportional representation of course solves none of the problems advanced here, for it simply pushes these problems and other ones as well into the lap of the legislature.

12. For example, suppose there are three individuals or groups, A, B, and C, and three alternatives, x, y, and z; and let their preferences be as follows:

The requirement that a vote be taken on every pair of alternatives perceived to exist, whether in an election or in choosing among motions in a legislative body or committee, is rarely if ever followed in the actual conduct of democratic organizations. Technical requirements for perfecting the arithmetical attainment of the Rule impose high costs in time, patience, understanding, and agreement that may well outweigh any perceived benefits in the real world. However, except for proportional representation, it is only fair to say that the practical application of rules necessary to achieve the majority principle is a subject that has not been of much interest to political scientists and other technicians in the past half-century; it may be that further examination would reveal some practical methods for meeting the fourth objection.

IV

In order to consider some of the ethical objections to populistic theory let us compare it briefly with the Madisonian argument. The essential assertion of the argument described in this chapter is that, given popular sovereignty and political equality as the only goals, it

---

A prefers x to y and y to z.

B prefers y to z and z to x.

C prefers z to y and y to x.

Now if each group votes according to its preferences, on the pair (x, y) the alternative y will be favored 2–1; if y is now paired with z, y will be favored 2–1 again. Clearly y is the most preferred alternative of a majority. Hence the choice of y will accord with the preferences of a 2–1 majority.

But now let us suppose that Group C does not vote on each pair according to its real preferences but rather to manipulate the final outcome in its favor. Thus, on the pair (x, y), although Group C actually prefers y to x, suppose that it casts its votes for x, which now wins this pair, 2–1. Then when x is paired with z, Group C votes its real preference; now z wins, 2–1. Ordinarily, since both x and y have been defeated in the voting and z has emerged with a $\frac{2}{3}$ majority, the voting would stop. Yet in this case a $\frac{2}{3}$ majority actually prefer a defeated alternative, y, to the winner z. Therefore, unless the body is given an opportunity to vote on the pair (y, z), the alternative that is selected, by a $\frac{2}{3}$ majority, will actually represent a choice that a $\frac{2}{3}$ majority would reject if given an opportunity to vote on the pair (y, z). Hence in this case, the Rule is not satisfied unless a vote is taken on *each* pair of alternatives.

Here again, transitivity leads to irrational conclusions, as just shown, and must be rejected in the real world. Cf. the discussion in Arrow, *op. cit.*, pp. 80–81, n. 8; Duncan Black, "The Decisions of a Committee Using a Special Majority," *Econometrics*, XVI (July, 1948), 245–61; and "On the Rationale of Group Decision-making," *Journal of Political Economy*, LVI (February, 1948), 23–34.

ought to be a necessary and sufficient condition for government policy that it accords with the preferences of the greater number of citizens (voters, or legislators). As against this, the Madisonian argument asserts, as an ethical inference from its basic assumptions, that accordance with the preferences of the greater number of citizens ought to be a necessary condition but not a sufficient condition for government policy. That is, the fact that a given policy is preferred by a majority to all known alternatives does not imply that the policy is actually adopted by the government; for external checks on the majority may prevent the alternative from being enacted as governmental policy.

Now on what grounds could one defend the desirability of the Rule as against Madison's propositions? In effect the question is: Why are political equality and popular sovereignty desirable? To undertake an exhaustive inquiry into these ethical questions, which in turn demands some theory about the validation of ethical propositions, is beyond my purposes here; for the examination of alternative democratic theories would soon turn into a subordinate element in a general critique of alternative ethical theories. Nevertheless, it might be desirable to sketch the general outline such a critique might take.

Historically the case for political equality and popular sovereignty has usually been deduced from beliefs in natural rights. But the assumptions that made the idea of natural rights intellectually defensible have tended to dissolve in modern times. Unless it is simply an elliptical mode of argument that might be cast in more precise language, the logic of natural rights seems to require a transcendental view in which the right is "natural" because God directly or indirectly wills it. God wills it as a right men ought to be (but not necessarily are) permitted by their fellows to exercise in society. It is easy to see that such an argument inevitably involves a variety of assumptions that at best are difficult and at worst impossible to prove to the satisfaction of anyone of positivist or skeptical predispositions.

The difficulty of deriving a more or less unchallengeable proof of the desirability of political equality and popular sovereignty directly from a transcendental ethic suggests the possibility of turning to proofs of an instrumentalist character. These at least postpone the problem of an ultimate justification, although of course they do not eliminate it for those who believe in the need for such an ultimate.

For example, if as a result of social indoctrination one feels anxieties in situations of political inequality; and if populistic democracy relieves these anxieties and does not create others of equal or greater severity, and if one prefers serenity to anxiety, then it would be rational to prefer populistic democracy to Madisonian democracy (or, of course, to dictatorship or any other hierarchical system). Because this kind of hedonism, even in our culture, seems to lack the psychological authority or acceptability of a transcendental ethic, the argument would be unsatisfactory to many individuals. Certainly it would not postpone the basic ethical question for long.

One might also attempt to demonstrate that in a given time and place, for historical and cultural reasons, no ethical rules other than those embodied in popular sovereignty and political equality would convey legitimacy to governmental decisions. And if legitimacy of governmental decisions could be shown to be necessary to a variety of goals, such as stability, then populistic democracy would be instrumentally necessary. But if, as we have been assuming, Madisonian democracy is the prevailing view in the United States, the argument would hardly apply to this country. The most that might be shown is that Americans have been indoctrinated to believe in both Madisonian and populistic democracy; that they have never fully reconciled the two; and that this failure robs governmental decisions of considerable legitimacy. It would be difficult to show, however, that a full shift to populistic democracy would therefore increase the legitimacy of governmental decisions.[13]

A third instrumentalist argument might be based upon a broad strategy for achieving a variety of one's goals. It is derived from the prediction that at least for one's self or the groups one supports the probability of maximizing a variety of highly ranked goals is higher in a populistic democracy than in any alternative to it. This assumes, of course, some given time and place, such as the United States in

13. Legitimacy is used here not in an ethical but in a psychological sense, i.e., a belief in the rightness of the decision or the process of decision-making.

1956, and it assumes some data, impressionistic or otherwise, on which to base a crude estimate of the probabilities. In this case one's commitment to populistic democracy is, from the logical point of view, entirely tentative; it is contingent upon the production of (or probability of producing) certain results. In actual practice, however, a viable system of democracy would undoubtedly require extensive social indoctrination and habituation.[14] Hence, although the commitment might be intellectually regarded as tentative, behaviorally it would need to be, and probably would be for most people, highly stable and powerfully anchored in the unconscious. In effect, then, it would be logically tentative but behaviorally much more rigid.

Let us follow the third argument further. Let us now rephrase our question this way. First, assume that Proposition 1 provides a rule with some positive probability of being used for governmental decisions, say in the United States. Next, assume that our sole criterion for choosing one rule or another is the probable effect of the rule on our goals or those of some other distinguishable group. Now, how can we rationally decide whether a rule maximizing popular sovereignty and political equality is preferable to "limited popular sovereignty" expressed in rules appropriate to Madisonian democracy? The answer obviously requires a very considerable amount of prediction as to the consequences of each. But the relations established by Definitions 1–3 and Proposition 1 are purely logical relations; they enable us to make no predictions whatsoever. That is, we have done no more than to establish a logical system which, however satisfying its logical symmetry, tells us nothing about the real world. Yet we cannot sensibly decide whether we prefer populistic to Madisonian democracy without estimating the probable consequences of each alternative if applied at some given time to some given group in the real world. Consequently we must turn to empirical observation for our answer. But to turn to empirical observation is to alter the whole problem from one of establishing purely logical relations to one of establishing empirical relations as well. We shall return to this point in Section V.

To be sure, the philosopher will say that we cannot prove the desir-

14. Cf. chap. 3.

ability of Proposition 1 entirely from empirical propositions—sooner or later we must make some basic ethical assumptions. Nevertheless, we shall not pursue the ultimate ethics of political equality and popular sovereignty any further. Instead, let us turn to some prior questions.

V

Even assuming that the approach suggested by the last argument is valid, one objection to populistic democracy is that it ignores differences in intensity of preference. In the language of economics, it rejects interpersonal comparisons of utilities. Suppose that it is possible for us to measure or, at least to order, intensities of preference. Suppose that x is only slightly preferred to y by a majority, and y is strongly preferred to x by a minority. The definition of political equality does not take this fact into account, and the Rule ignores it. Hence, in such a case even if the majority exceeds the minority only by one, populistic democracy, as we have seen, would nevertheless require the majority's choice to be government policy. It is perhaps the fear that occasionally a quite highly ranked goal might be invaded by a diffident majority that causes even the most ardent American democrats so frequently to prefer Madisonian to populistic democracy—at least for the United States.

In order to deal with this problem, we must turn briefly to Proposition 2, which we have so far ignored. This, the condition of "last say," holds that "populistic democracy is desirable, at least for governmental decisions, at least as a final appeal when other specified processes have been exhausted, and at least among adult citizens." The argument for this condition is as follows. Although the rules of populistic democracy can be extended to many types of organizations, government is the most crucial organization. The condition is therefore intended to insure that populistic democracy applies at least to government. Government is crucial because its controls are relatively powerful. In a wide variety of situations, in a contest between governmental controls and other controls, the governmental controls will probably prove more decisive than competing controls. To be sure, the effectiveness of governmental controls is limited; it would be easy to exaggerate their comparative strength; nevertheless, political history is a record of bitter and often sanguinary struggles to control the controls we call governmental. It is reasonable to assume that in a variety of policy-making situations whoever controls governmental decisions will have significantly greater control over policy than individuals who do not control governmental decisions. Hence the argument for populistic democracy is initially, at least, an argument for populistic democracy in government.

But the phrase "populistic democracy in government" can be misleading. "Government" includes many types of social process; the bureaus are hierarchical, some of them operate within a price system, and bargaining among hierarchical leaders is common. The demand for populistic democracy does not entail a demand for the elimination of all of these alternative control processes in government. Just as government is a crucial system of controls within a society, so within government the processes that allow a more or less final or decisive voice on policy are crucial. Hence the argument for populistic democracy applies to these crucial processes within government where the "last say" may be had.

The restriction of the "last say" to adults is defended on a variety of grounds; although the most desirable lower age limit is moderately controversial the basic principle is so little contested that I do not propose to review the arguments for it.

Now let us turn back to the question of intensities. Even an individual who finds the Rule reasonable in cases where he believes the intensity of desire is about the same among the individuals in the minority and majority might find it intolerable in the type of case cited above, where x is only slightly preferred by a bare majority and y is very strongly preferred by a bare minority. Indeed, probably no one would advocate the Rule for every situation. The real question is whether one advocates it (a) for government, (b) as a final appeal, (c) among adults, i.e., whether one wants it even in the "last say."

Suppose someone denies the validity of the Rule even under the condition of last say, on the ground that it does not adequately reflect intensities of desire. To deny the Rule is to say either that no rule is valid, which would be of little help in the real world, or that a contrary rule is valid. A contrary rule would have to assert that in some cases where the desire of the minority for *y* is more intense than the desire of a majority for *x*, governmental policy must follow minority preference rather than majority preference (the Qualified Minority Rule).

To make this rule operational, one would need to specify a method for deciding when a particular instance falls within this category. Suppose one permits the majority to decide. At first sight this seems senseless and indeed logically contradictory; but in fact, it happens frequently in democratic countries, whether operating under Madisonian rules or something like the principle of majority rule. There is a variety of reasons why a majority that initially has only a slight preference for a policy might finally accede to the demands of an intense minority; the intensity of the desires of other people, and the probable political actions resulting from different degrees of intensity, are among the factors that many individuals, and certainly many political leaders, might take into account in deciding their own policy preferences.

But suppose that this kind of solution, which is entirely compatible with the Rule, is held to be inadequate, since the final decision still lies with the majority. Then the Qualified Minority Rule must be made operational by specifying a particular minority that could be trusted to invoke its power in cases, but only in those cases, where the intensity of a minority's preference for *y* was significantly greater than the intensity of a majority's preference for *x*. Unfortunately, as we shall see in chapter 4, in the real world it is difficult to construct deliberately an official organization appropriate to this requirement. Philosopher kings are hard to come by.

VI

A final and I believe valid ethical objection to the theory of populistic democracy is that it postulates only two goals to be maximized—political equality and popular sovereignty. Yet no one, except perhaps a fanatic, wishes to maximize two goals at the expense of all others. Hence any political ethic that lays down rules suitable only to the attainment of one or two goals is inadequate for most of us.

For most of us—and this may be particularly true in countries that have managed to operate democracies over long periods of time—the costs of pursuing any one or two goals at the expense of others are thought to be excessive. Most of us are marginalists. Generally we experience diminishing marginal utility the more we attain any one goal; or in the language of contemporary psychology, goal attainment reduces the drive value of the stimulus. Political equality and popular sovereignty are not absolute goals; we must ask ourselves how much leisure, privacy, consensus, stability, income, security, progress, status, and probably many other goals we are prepared to forego for an additional increment of political equality. It is an observable fact that almost no one regards political equality and popular sovereignty as worth an unlimited sacrifice of these other goals.

Would populistic democracy impose costs in, say, the kinds of goals listed above? This is a question to which the theory provides no answer. Yet surely a theory that does not indicate the probable costs against which probable gains must be measured is too incomplete to assist us much in the real world.

VII

The last remark recalls a point made earlier: the theory of populistic democracy is not an empirical system. It consists only of logical relations among ethical postulates. It tells us nothing about the real world. From it we can predict no behavior whatsoever.

This is a point of cardinal importance in appraising the significance of the theory. For as we have seen, on a number of issues it is difficult or impossible for us to decide what rule we would prefer to follow until we have predicted the probable consequences of employing the Rule in the real world. But here the theory of populistic democracy is of no assistance. It does not tell us how to approximate or maximize popular sovereignty and political equality in the real world. It simply tells us that perfect attainment of these conditions, assuming them to be attainable, would require us to pursue the Rule. But this is rarely if ever the shape of an ethical problem in the real world, and I believe it is never so in politics.

There is a great variety of empirical facts that one needs to know, or have some hunches about, before one can rationally decide on the kinds of political rules one wants to follow in the real world. Moreover, the factual situation might well vary from time to time and from one social organization to another. Thus, even if one's goals (values) remain stable, a set of rules that will maximize the attainment of these goals in one situation might be entirely unsuitable in another. Surely there is no a priori reason for supposing that populistic democracy would maximize one's goals (or the goals of others) in every culture, society, and time. Hence even if one believes that political equality and popular sovereignty are desirable goals (among others), evidently the relevant question needs to be posed something like this: Would some specific proposal (e.g., elimination of judicial review, or unified political parties, or changes in the lengths of terms of office, or adoption of a parliamentary system, etc.), if adopted in, say, the United States today, more nearly approximate to these two goals than existing or other alternative arrangements, and at the same time not impose excessive costs to other values? To answer such a question it is clear that one must go outside the theory of populistic democracy to empirical political science.

In chapter 3 we shall examine some of the most important empirical relationships that seem to exist in political systems that are called democratic (at least in the West). In the remainder of this chapter, I shall concern myself with three objections to the theory of populistic democracy that raise significant empirical questions.

First, the theory does not indicate what individuals or groups should be included in the political system to which political equality, popular sovereignty, and the Rule are to apply. No doubt some advocates of populistic democracy would like to see every human being living in such a system; but so far as I know, no political theorist has ever advocated a single, world-wide system of populistic democracy. Historically modern democracy and nationalism developed roughly during the same period, and modern democratic theorists have usually explicitly or implicitly proposed the system for the nation state. Some, like Rousseau, seem to have considered it suitable for small groups about the size of a canton; Jefferson evidently thought of political equality and popular sovereignty as more workable at the state level than in the federal government, where in practice he accepted the Madisonian system. The question remains, however: Should one set of individuals be included rather than another? So far as I am aware, no democratic theorist has provided us with any systematic answer to this question.

It might be said that the appropriate boundaries would include only individuals who agree to the Rule. But surely this would make the system unworkable in the real world. For since geographical boundaries are probably required as a practical matter, is it likely that any significant geographical area includes only individuals who agree to the Rule? If it is then urged that the boundaries should include groups within which a majority agrees to the Rule, it turns out that this rule provides us with no operationally useful principle at all. For how is such a decision to be arrived at in the real world? Suppose the area known as Greater Wysteria is found to have a majority of adults who agree to the Rule; but of the minority who oppose the Rule, enough live in the section of Greater Wysteria known as South Wysteria to compose a majority in that section. Hence our tentative principle tells us both to draw the boundaries around Greater Wysteria and to exclude South Wysteria, that is, it is a self-contradictory instruction.

Bounds of inclusion and exclusion for geographical governmental units are, in the real world, among the most rigid of political phenomena. One does not need to call on the experiences of nation states for evidence; it is sufficient to note the difficulties that nearly always bar the way of proposals for urban consolidation. To a great extent, everyone must take the boundaries of his political world as given by prior tradition and historical events. Such boundaries are not often open to rational change.

Even if they were open to rational change, for any individual with many values, rather than merely the two embodied in political equality and popular sovereignty, the most rational rule to follow would appear to be something like this: Select a political society that contains individuals whose goals are sufficiently like your own to provide the highest probability that you will maximize all your key values. Because political equality and popular sovereignty are only two values. it would be quite rational for an individual to sacrifice some of these to insure the attainment of others. Hence he might well find it rational to select boundaries that would include individuals, perhaps a majority of individuals, who favored Madisonian democracy or even some other alternative political system. Thus the Connecticut Compromise is not necessarily a foolish compromise even to those Americans who place a very high value on political equality and hence disapprove of equal state representation in the Senate. For it may well be far and away the best all-around bargain an American can get in the real world; i.e., any realistic alternative would be less satisfactory.

Whether this is or is not the case, I am not arguing here; the point is that the theory of populistic democracy does not provide any satisfactory criteria for deciding who should be included in the system. To develop such satisfactory criteria requires careful attention to a host of empirical facts that are not specified in the system and, indeed, could not be without converting it from a system of pure logic to an empirical theory.

VIII

A second empirical problem is posed by Gaetano Mosca, whose objection can be paraphrased as follows: Every society develops a ruling class. Widespread popular control (certainly rule by a majority) is impossible. However, the extent to which a ruling class is sensitive to popular desires and responsive to election returns depends to some extent upon the constitutional system, the prevailing ideology, and social indoctrination. Doctrines and constitutional procedures providing for absolute popular sovereignty and majority rule provide the weakest checks of all on the rulers. For, since the majority will not rule in any case, doctrines and procedures of this kind in effect grant unlimited power to the ruling minority, who of course claim to represent the majority. Hence nowhere is tyranny more likely than in a society where the constitutional system and the prevailing ideology legitimize the unlimited constitutional power of the majority.

Mosca's objection, it should be pointed out, can scarcely give comfort to Madisonian critics of populistic democracy. For the objection rests upon the explicit assumption that the whole idea of majority tyranny is preposterous; the majority never rules, and consequently it can never tyrannize; only minorities rule, and consequently tyranny is always carried on by minorities.

I shall not attempt to decide in this chapter[15] whether or not Mosca's objection is valid. The important point is that Mosca's objection raises a host of empirical questions for which the theory of populistic democracy provides no answer.

IX

A third empirical problem has been the source of considerable intellectual confusion, in large part, perhaps, because of linguistic ambiguities. This problem arises from the objection that under a system of popular sovereignty, political equality, and majority rule, a majority might well take actions that would destroy the system; hence some method of minority veto may be necessary to prevent this. In the United States a variety of elements in the constitutional system provide a minority veto, including the Supreme Court, the composition of the Senate, the congressional committee system, the filibuster, and at times, perhaps, the presidency.[16]

15. Cf. chapter 5, pp. 124 ff.

16. Because part of the problem is purely verbal, let me employ once more a simple notational system to summarize the steps in the argument. The conditions of popular sovereignty and political equality, it will be recalled, are satisfied only if

$$x \, Pg \, y \leftrightarrow NP(x, y) > NP(y, x) . \tag{1}$$

In order to simplify the discussion that follows, let the symbol ma stand for the set of all voters greater than $N/2$, and mi the set of all voters less than $N/2$. (For reasons already discussed, we shall avoid situations where the majority is undefined, i.e., where $NP(x, y) = NP(y, x)$.) Now (1) can be written simply as

$$x \, Pma \, y \leftrightarrow x \, Pg \, y . \tag{2}$$

Let us define the *condition of minority veto* as follows:

$$x \, Pma \, y \rightarrow x \, Pg \, y \text{ if and only if } x \, Pmi \, y . \tag{3}$$

It is important to distinguish (3) from a rather different situation which I shall call the *condition of oligarchy;* it is defined as follows:

Take x^* as some key prerequisite to political equality and popular sovereignty, say, some measure of freedom of speech. Let us assume that y is an alternative that would reduce freedom of speech to the point where popular sovereignty is impossible and oligarchy inevitable.[17] It might be argued that a minority veto is necessary to prevent the enactment of y and with it the destruction not merely of populistic democracy itself but of any real world approximation to it.

The problem becomes complicated at this point by the need to take into account the time period within which popular preferences are expected to be translated into governmental policy. No advocate of populistic democracy, so far as I am aware, has ever demanded an instantaneous translation of majority preferences into government policies; that is, some time lag is assumed to exist between the first occurrence of majority preference and the government action carrying it out. Advocates of democracy have generally supposed that the

$$x \; Pmi \; y \rightarrow x \; Pg \; y \text{ even if } y \; Pma \; x \,. \tag{4}$$

Minority veto and oligarchy are not identical, for it is not true that in all cases under the condition of minority veto the minority preference becomes government policy. On the contrary, in some cases the preference of the minority becomes policy only when it coincides with the preference of the majority, i.e., (3) may also be stated as follows:

$$x \; Pmi \; y \rightarrow x \; Pg \; y \text{ if and only if } x \; Pma \; y \,. \tag{5}$$

Now the objection which we are examining asserts that a minority veto over actions of a majority may sometimes prevent democratic government from slipping into pure oligarchy, as defined by (4). There are, however, some serious difficulties in this argument.

In the first place, although it is true that the condition of oligarchy is not identical with the condition of minority veto, in all situations where the minority with the veto prefers existing policy and a majority prefers an alternative to existing policy, the difference between oligarchy and minority veto vanishes. Let x^* represent existing policy. Then, by (3)

$$y \; Pma \; x^* \rightarrow y \; Pg \; x^* \text{ if and only if } y \; Pmi \; x^* \,. \tag{6}$$

But if the minority with a veto does in fact prefer x^*, which is existing policy, and can veto y, which is an alternative to it, then

$$x^* \; Pmi \; y \rightarrow x^* \; Pg \; y \text{ even if } y \; Pma \; x^* \,. \tag{7}$$

Because (7) is identical with (4), in these circumstances the condition of minority veto is identical with the condition of oligarchy.

17. The question might properly be raised: In whose opinion will these consequences occur? Here we encounter again some of the intellectual difficulties of the Madisonian system discussed above.

majority choice ought to be a reflective one; rational choice requires knowledge of one's own values, technical knowledge about the alternatives, and knowledge about the probable consequences of each alternative. Such knowledge, it has traditionally been held, requires time for debate, discussion, hearings, and other time-consuming devices.

How long a delay is compatible with the Rule? The theory of populistic democracy provides no answer; it is a static system, not one con-

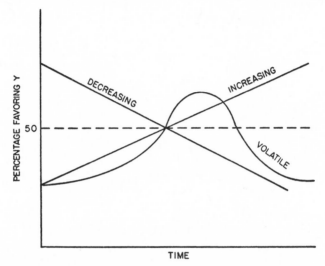

Fig. 1.—Three possible states of public opinion concerning alternative Y

structed on a time sequence. If one month is compatible, why not two? Why not a year, two years, ten? To say that the delay should be long enough for a rational choice to be formed is useless because it is a counsel of perfection; or, if not that, it is operationally meaningless. Nevertheless, such a reply suggests several types of situations and a complete theory would need to account for them.

One kind of situation exists when opinion in favor of *y* declines steadily from a majority to a minority; another exists when opinion is volatile—the majority in favor of *y* is short-lived; a third exists when opinion in favor of *y* increases steadily over time. The figure above represents these three possibilities (Fig. 1).

Now if opinion in favor of y (a policy that would lead to oligarchy) is declining or volatile, then the minority veto exercised in favor of x^* produces oligarchy in the short run, but not necessarily in the long run.[18] But if, after due reflection, a majority concludes that it has been mistaken and really prefers x^* to y, then as a result of the minority veto it can continue to operate under the minority veto system, which is certainly not oligarchy.[19]

However, if opinion in favor of y is growing over the long run, then every solution leads to oligarchy. To operate under populistic democracy will produce oligarchy; for under our assumptions the choice of y is a *de facto* choice for oligarchy. Alternatively, the minority veto will lead to oligarchy.[20]

It should be said, however, that whereas the first case might produce oligarchy in all governmental decisions, in the second case the condition of oligarchy might be restricted to the particular case. Certainly there is an important difference between these two situations, although neither is populistic democracy.

So far in this argument we have been operating without facts. Yet we cannot evaluate the objection posed here until we have tried to predict the probability of the events which the minority veto is said to forestall. Moreover, we would want to know whether a minority could be found capable of exercising its veto in such cases and not simply using its powers to establish oligarchy in all situations where the status quo is being challenged. These predictions cannot be derived analytically. They require empirical study of a particular culture, time, and place.

Americans are inclined to believe that the Supreme Court is the *deus ex machina* that regularly saves American democracy from itself. This view is difficult to support by the actual decisions of the Court. The Court performs some indispensable functions by means of judicial

18. That is, in the short run:

$$x^* \; Pmi \; y \rightarrow x^* \; Pg \; y \text{ even if } y \; Pma \; x^*, \tag{8}$$

which is identical with (4) or oligarchy.

19. In the sense that (3) and (5) in n. 16 are not equivalent to (4).

20. The long-run situation is that of Proposition (7) in n. 16, which is oligarchy.

review, but preventing national majorities from destroying key pre-requisites of political democracy is not one of them. I assume that the "key prerequisites to political equality and popular sovereignty" are the right to vote, freedom of speech, freedom of assembly, and freedom of the press. In its entire history, on seventy-seven occasions the Supreme Court has held acts of Congress unconstitutional. Of these, only twelve can be properly characterized as involving non-economic civil liberties. Of these twelve, six involved the efforts of the Congress to protect and extend the rights of Negroes. In all six cases the Supreme Court vetoed this attempt to convey to the freed slaves approximately the same formal rights as are enjoyed by white citizens. Of the twelve cases, only four—all dealing with the rights of Negroes—may reasonably be interpreted as involving one or more of the key prerequisites referred to above. In the only four cases in the entire history of the Court where legislation dealing with the key prerequisites has been held unconstitutional, then, the decisions prevented Congress, not from destroying basic rights, but from extending them. Thus, there is not a single case in the history of this nation where the Supreme Court has struck down national legislation designed to curtail, rather than to expand, the key prerequisites to popular equality and popular sovereignty.[21]

In this instance, as in all others where factual information is required, the theory of populistic democracy provides us with no knowledge about the real world. I may prefer political equality to inequality and popular sovereignty to oligarchy, just as I may prefer a society

21. Cf. Library of Congress, Provisions of Federal Law Held Unconstitutional by the Supreme Court of the United States, Washington, 1936. The only additional case since that time involving Congressional legislation has been *United States* v. *Lovett*, 328 U.S. 303 (1936). On the point made above, see especially Commager, *op. cit.*, p. 55. John D. Frank comes to the same conclusion, although he tabulates the cases somewhat differently. He finds nineteen cases that had to do with civil liberties. Of these, eight were "peripheral"; of the remaining eleven cases, eight limited liberty, three aided it. The eight were decisions involving rights of Negroes. Frank, however, infers from these facts that the Court should intervene more positively in legislation involving civil liberties, an inference not involved in the argument of this chapter. See "Review and Basic Liberties," in *Supreme Court and Supreme Law*, ed. Edmund N. Cahn (Bloomington: Indiana University Press, 1954).

without murder to one where I live in "continual fear and danger of violent death." But until I have made a whole host of predictions about events in the real world, my preferences do not enable me to decide what, if anything, I should do to reduce violent death in my society. Neither do they enable me to make rational choices among alternative political arrangements, some of which may have an impact on political equality and popular sovereignty.

Does this mean, then, that we can wash our hands of political equality? Is it a stupid goal because much of democratic theory is, properly analyzed, irrelevant to the real world? Obviously this is not so.

If the Madisonian compromise is unsatisfactory, we do not need to be driven back in desperation to an axiomatic body of theory that is, in the end, almost useless as a guide to action. For there is nothing inherent in the concept of political equality that makes it devoid of meaning in the real world.

APPENDIX TO CHAPTER 2

The proof of Proposition 1

That the principle of majority rule (Proposition 1) is already contained in the definition of populistic democracy (Definitions 1–3) seems to me intuitively obvious; it is only at the risk of presenting an essentially trivial demonstration of the logical relations involved that I submit the following proof.

Following the notational system in the footnotes, we have already seen that the Definition of the Rule (Definition 4) may be stated as:

DEFINITION 4': $NP(x, y) > NP(y, x) \leftrightarrow x\, Pg\, y$.

Now let us see what our task is: We must somehow interpret the conditions of popular sovereignty and political equality so that they are compatible one with the other. Definition 2 tells us that the condition of popular sovereignty is satisfied if:

$$x\, Pc\, y \leftrightarrow x\, Pg\, y, \tag{1}$$

where Pc means "preferred by the members."

But how shall we decide what alternative is "preferred" or "most preferred" by the members? What rule shall we follow to give operational meaning to the expression $(x\, Pc\, y)$ or the concept "alternative most preferred by the members"? Can we, for example, take differing intensities of prefer-

ence into account? In chapter 4 we shall see what a host of formidable difficulties arise in any attempt to consider intensities. Meanwhile it is clear
that the interpretation we give to (1) must be consistent with the condition
of political equality, else we shall not be able to satisfy both conditions.
It appears to be consistent with, and indeed necessary to, the condition of
political equality that preferences should somehow be individually signified
by citizens in such a way that these preferences can be assigned values and
counted. Historically the casting of a vote has been accepted as an appropriate indicator of individual preferences. But if voting, or some other individual
action, is taken as an expression of preference, how are the votes to be
counted? Here the condition of political equality evidently requires that we
ignore intensities because the preference of each member is assigned an
equal value. That is, we must count votes in such a way that:

$$V' = V'' = V''' \ldots \text{etc.,} \tag{2}$$

where V' stands for the vote of one individual, V'' of another, etc. But in
order to follow this rule, the ordinary properties of the real numbers must
be invoked, so that the following condition is satisfied by the process of
counting:

$$1 V < 2 V < 3 V < 4 V \ldots \text{etc.} \tag{3}$$

$$n V < (n+1) V \tag{4}$$

$$\frac{n V}{2} < \frac{n V}{2} + 1 V, \quad \text{and} \quad \frac{n V}{2} < \frac{(n+1) V}{2}. \tag{5}$$

That is, to be compatible with Definition 3, "most preferred" must be compatible with (2) to (5). Hence:

$$NP (x, y) > NP (y, x) \leftrightarrow x P c y. \tag{6}$$

But since, by (1),

$$x P c y \leftrightarrow x P g y$$

then by substitution

$$NP (x, y) > NP (y, x) \leftrightarrow x P g y. \tag{7}$$

But (7) is precisely the meaning of Definitions 4 and 4'.

Definition of majority

It is worth noting that if (7) is adhered to in all situations, then even a
bare majority would be sufficient to establish government policy, i.e.,

$$\frac{N+1}{2} P (x, y) \quad \text{and} \quad \frac{N-1}{2} P (y, x) \rightarrow x P g y.$$

To correspond with reality, a bare majority can be differently defined depending on whether the total number of citizens (or votes) is odd or even. It is therefore convenient to define "majority" as meaning:

$$\frac{N}{2} + 1 \text{ or greater in all cases where } N \text{ is even.}$$

$$\frac{N+1}{2} \text{ or greater in all cases where } N \text{ is odd.}$$

CHAPTER 3

Polyarchal
Democracy

I

Examination of Madisonian and populistic theory suggests at least two possible methods one might employ to construct a theory of democracy. One way, the method of maximization, is to specify a set of goals to be maximized; democracy can then be defined in terms of the specific governmental processes necessary to maximize these goals or some among them. The two theories we have been considering are essentially of this type: Madisonian theory postulates a non-tyrannical republic as the goal to be maximized; populistic theory postulates popular sovereignty and political equality. A second way—this one might be called the descriptive method—is to consider as a single class of phenomena all those nation states and social organizations that are commonly called democratic by political scientists, and by examining the members of this class to discover, first, the distinguishing characteristics they have in common, and, second, the necessary and sufficient conditions for social organizations possessing these characteristics.

These are not, however, mutually exclusive methods. And we shall see that if we begin by employing the first method it will soon become necessary to employ something rather like the second as well.

II

We discovered in chapter 2 that the goals of populistic democracy and the simple Rule deduced from these goals do not provide us with anything like a complete theory. One basic defect of the theory is that it does no more than to provide a formal redefinition of one necessary procedural rule for the perfect or ideal attainment of political equality and popular sovereignty; but because the theory is no more than an exercise in axiomatics, it tells us nothing about the real world. However, let us now pose the key question in slightly different form: What are the necessary and sufficient conditions for maximizing democracy in the real world? I shall show that the words "in the real world" fundamentally alter the problem.

Let us begin, however, with a meticulous concern for precision of meaning. First, what do we mean by "maximizing democracy"? Evidently here, as in populistic theory, we must proceed by regarding democracy as a state of affairs constituting a limit, and all actions approaching the limit will be maximizing actions. But how shall we describe the state of affairs constituting the limit?

The model of populistic democracy suggests three possible characteristics that might be made operationally meaningful: (1) Whenever policy choices are perceived to exist, the alternative selected and enforced as governmental policy is the alternative most preferred by the members. (2) Whenever policy choices are perceived to exist, in the process of choosing the alternative to be enforced as government policy, the preference of each member is assigned an equal value. (3) The Rule: In choosing among alternatives, the alternative preferred by the greater number is selected.

To make the first of these operational we must either ignore the problem of different intensities of preference among individuals or find ourselves in so deep a morass of obstacles to observation and comparison that it would be very nearly impossible to say whether or not the characteristic in fact exists. I shall return to this problem in the next chapter. But if we ignore intensities, then in effect we adopt the second characteristic as our criterion: that the preference of each member is assigned an equal value. It would appear at first glance that the question whether the preference of each member of an organization is assigned an equal value is more or less susceptible of observation. Likewise the third characteristic, the Rule, should be observable. But since the Rule is deducible from the first two characteristics, would it not be enough simply to examine a social organization in order to discover the extent to which the Rule is or is not followed? That is, do we have in the Rule an adequate definition of the limit of democracy? Suppose we observe that a majority prefers x to y, and x happens to be selected as government policy. Yet it may be that among the majority is a dictator; if he were in the minority, then y would be selected. The condition of political equality evidently requires "interchangeability," i.e., the interchange of an equal number of individuals from one side to another would not affect the outcome of the decision. But how can we observe whether interchangeability is present? Evidently no single decision provides us with enough information, for at best a single decision can only reveal that the Rule is not being followed and that political equality therefore does not exist during that decision. We can infer interchangeability only by examining a large number of cases. What can we actually observe even in a large number of decisions?

Suppose we observe that when A is with a majority, the majority choice is made the policy of the organization; and when A is with a minority, the minority choice becomes policy. Evidently interchangeability is violated. But what we have observed is nothing more than the extent to which the Rule is employed in more than one case. So far, then, the concept "political equality" does not suggest a set of observations other than those necessary to determine whether the Rule is or is not followed.

Now let us suppose that A is always with the majority and the majority choice is always enforced as policy. Yet we suspect that if A were with a minority, the minority choice would be enforced. What observations must we now make to determine whether or not our hunch is correct? Here we come to an important conclusion: If we take any specific action, such as the outcome of balloting, as a satisfactory index of preference, then no operational tests exist for determining political equality, other than those necessary for determining whether the Rule is or is not being followed. That is, given the expression of preferences as adequate, the only operational test for political equality is the extent to which the Rule is followed in a number of cases. Hence, assuming the validity of the expressed preferences, one can never properly speak of a particular decision as "democratic" but only of a series of decisions. (One can, of course, properly specify a particular decision as not democratic.) Hence our key question now becomes: What events must we observe in the real world in order to determine the extent to which the Rule is employed in an organization?

Unfortunately, the phrase "given the expression of preferences" harbors some serious difficulties. What kinds of activity shall we take as indices of preference? At one extreme we could rely on some overt act of choosing, such as casting a ballot or making a statement.[1] At the other extreme, through deep and careful probing we could search for psychological evidence. If the first is often naïve, the second is impossible on a sufficient scale. In practice most of us adopt a middle course and take our clues from the prevailing environment in which the particular preference is expressed. In one environment we accept the overt act of voting as an adequate if imperfect index; in another we reject it entirely.

Therefore it is of crucial importance to specify the particular stage in the decision process at which we propose to take the expression of preference as given. It is entirely consistent to say that at one stage the Rule is employed, and hence at that level the decision is definitionally "democratic"; and at the same time to say that at another stage the Rule is not employed and the decision at that stage is not democratic. In the actual world of governmental politics in the United States, the only stage at which the Rule is at all closely approximated seems to be during vote counting in elections and legislative bodies. In the prevoting stage many influences, including those of superior wealth and control over organizational resources, so greatly exaggerate the power of the few as compared with the many that the social processes leading up to the process of voting may properly be spoken of as highly inegalitarian and undemocratic, although less so than in a dictatorship.[2]

1. More accurately, in using votes and opinion polls we generally rely on some overt statements of individuals who compile the returns.

2. It is conceivable that the converse could exist, i.e., a dictatorship that rejected the Rule at the voting level but organized the society so that the prevoting stages of decision-making were highly democratic. But I am unaware of such a society. Sympathetic Western interpreters of Soviet communism have sometimes suggested

Thus there is possible in democratic theory a kind of finite regression to different stages in the decision process; but so long as one is quite clear as to which stage one is describing, some of the common ambiguities can be avoided.

III

The effect of the argument so far is to divide our key question into two: (1) What acts shall we consider sufficient to constitute an expression of individual preferences at a given stage in the decision process? (2) Taking these acts as an expression of preferences, what events must we observe in order to determine the extent to which the Rule is employed in the organization we are examining? We are still looking, let us remember, for a set of limiting conditions to be approached.

At a minimum, two stages need to be distinguished: the election stage[3] and the interelection stage. The election stage in turn consists of at least three periods which it is useful to distinguish: the voting period, the prevoting period, and the postvoting period. (It would be possible to define the duration of these periods more precisely in particular cases but no general definition is likely to be very useful. Hence in what follows the duration of each is unspecified.)

During the voting period we would need to observe the extent to which at least three conditions exist:

1. Every member of the organization performs the acts we assume to constitute an expression of preference among the scheduled alternatives, e.g., voting.

2. In tabulating these expressions (votes), the weight assigned to the choice of each individual is identical.

3. The alternative with the greatest number of votes is declared the winning choice.

---

such a relationship there, but the evidence seems overwhelming that both the social structure and the decision process in politics are extremely inegalitarian. Something like this, however, seems to permeate the Webbs' curious picture of the U.S.S.R. in *Soviet Communism: A New Civilization?*

3. Election is used here in a broad sense. To apply the analysis to the internal operation of an organization that is itself constituted through elections, such as a legislative body, one would consider votes on measures as "the election stage."

The connection between these three conditions and the Rule is self-evident. If the act of expressing preferences is taken as given, then these conditions appear to constitute necessary and sufficient conditions for the operation of the Rule during the voting period.[4] But it is equally self-evident that we have thus far begged the first of our questions. A totalitarian plebiscite might meet—and indeed in practice evidently often has met—these three conditions better than a national election or legislative decision in countries that most Western political scientists would call democratic. The crux of the problem is in our first question, what we take to constitute an expression of individual preference. Can it not be truthfully said that the peasant who casts his ballot for the dictatorship is expressing his preferences among the scheduled alternatives as he sees them? For, perhaps, the alternatives he sees are either to vote for the dictatorship or to take a journey to Siberia. That is, in one sense, every human decision can be regarded as a conscious or unconscious choice of the preferred alternative among those perceived by the actor. Likewise, the most corrupt urban political machines in this country often meet these requirements when the ward-heelers do not actually stuff the ballot boxes or tamper with the returns; for they provide a sufficient number of unscrupulous hangers-on with a simple alternative: a few dollars if you vote our slate and nothing if you vote for the other side.

In a rough sense, the essence of all competitive politics is bribery of the electorate by politicians. How then shall we distinguish the vote of

4. Condition 1 must be interpreted with care, for the expression "acts" is open to ambiguity. Suppose that the members of the organization must choose between alternatives x and y; every member has a preference for one or the other; and the ratio of those who prefer x to those who prefer y is a/b. Then so long as those who actually vote do so in this ratio, the magnitude of the vote is not strictly relevant. All that is required for the Rule is that the voters be fully representative of all the members. Indeed, in a choice among only two alternatives, the Rule would be satisfied even more easily, for it would only require that if $a/b > 1$, then $a_1/b_1 > 1$, and if $a/b < 1$, then $a_1/b_1 < 1$, where a_1 is the number of voters who prefer x and b_1 the number of voters who prefer y. However, in terms of observables, by what "act" do we know the ratio a/b, if not by voting or some equivalent to it? So that if we are concerned with observables and do not require Condition 1 for the voting process itself, then we must require it for some prior act that we "assume to constitute an expression of preference among the scheduled alternatives" and on which the outcome of the voting itself is partly dependent.

the Soviet peasant or the bribed stumble-bum from the farmer who supports a candidate committed to high support prices, the business-man who supports an advocate of low corporation taxes, or the consumer who votes for candidates opposed to a sales tax? I assume that we wish to exclude expressions of preference of the first kind but to include the second. For if we do not exclude the first, then any distinction between totalitarian and democratic systems is fatuous; but if we exclude the second, then surely no examples of even the most proximate democracies can be found to exist anywhere. We can hardly afford to read the human race out of democratic politics.

This is a problem that calls for subtle distinctions, yet, so far as I am aware, it is not much treated in the literature. The distinction we seek is evidently not to be found in the magnitude of the rewards or deprivations resulting from the choice; the gain of the stumble-bum is paltry indeed, and by comparison with the gain of the large corporate stockholder it is microscopic. If we simply take as our criterion the magnitude of the possible deprivations for making a wrong choice,[5] then to be sure, one of the alternatives perceived by the Russian peasant may be more than human flesh and spirit were ever meant for; but by comparison the Western voter who perceives the alternatives among candidates as nuclear war or cold peace is not far removed from the plight of the Russian peasant.

What we balk at in accepting the vote of the Soviet citizen as an expression of preference is that he is not permitted to choose among all the alternatives that we, as outside observers, regard as in some sense potentially available to him. If he is faced with the alternatives: x vote for the ruling slate or y vote against the ruling slate, followed by living death in a concentration camp, his preference for x over y is as genuine as any you are likely to find in any election anywhere. But if he could schedule the alternatives to include z, vote against the ruling slate with no foreseeable punishment following, then we are more likely to accept the outcome of his choice among this set of alternatives, even if tne set

5. Some might propose that the test be based on the public v. private or social v. selfish quality of the choice. But analysis would show either that this distinction is meaningless or else that few, if any, cases of the former exist, i.e., if not meaningless the distinction is irrelevant to our problem.

is from our point of view by no means perfect. We might now expect him to prefer z to x and x to y; but if he stubbornly prefers x to z we are no longer on sound footing in rejecting the results of the plebiscite, if they otherwise conform to the three conditions set forth above.

What we have done, then, is to formulate a fourth limiting condition, one that must exist in the prevoting period governing the scheduling of alternatives for the voting period.

4. Any member who perceives a set of alternatives, at least one of which he regards as preferable to any of the alternatives presently scheduled, can insert his preferred alternative(s) among those scheduled for voting.

Even so, our problem is not entirely solved. For suppose that a group of voters is known to prefer x to y and y to z. But A, who prefers y to z and z to x, possesses a monopoly of information and persuades the other voters that x is not an available or relevant alternative. Hence no one proposes x and the voters choose y. All of our four conditions are complied with; yet most of us will not accept a prevoting period governed by this kind of monopoly control over information. Therefore we must lay down a fifth condition operating in the prevoting period.

5. All individuals possess identical information about the alternatives.

Perhaps three remarks need to be made. If one is dismayed by the Utopian character of the last two requirements, it is worth recalling that we are looking for conditions that may be used as limits against which real world achievement can actually be measured. Moreover, even if the fifth condition were to exist in full, voters might choose an alternative they would have rejected if they had possessed more information, i.e., the fifth condition is certainly no guarantee of cosmic rationality. At best it permits us to say that the choice has not been manipulated by controls over information possessed by any one individual or group. Finally, it must be admitted that the fourth and fifth conditions are by no means as easily observable as the first three; in practice the observer would be forced to accept some crude indices for the existence of these last two conditions, and, to this extent, the set of limiting conditions we intended to set out as observable must themselves be interpreted by still other unspecified phenomena susceptible of observation.

At first glance it might be thought that these five conditions are sufficient to guarantee the operation of the Rule; but, at least in principle, it would be possible for a regime to permit these conditions to operate through the prevoting and voting periods and then simply to ignore the results. Consequently, we must postulate at least two more conditions for the postvoting period both of which are sufficiently obvious to need no discussion:

6. Alternatives (leaders or policies) with the greatest number of votes displace any alternatives (leaders or policies) with fewer votes.

7. The orders of elected officials are executed.

These, then, constitute our set of more or less observable limiting conditions which when present during the election stage will be taken as evidence for the maximal operation of the Rule, which in turn is taken as evidence for the maximal attainment of political equality and popular sovereignty. What of the interelection stage? If our argument so far is correct, then maximization of political equality and popular sovereignty in the interelection stage would require:

8.1. Either that all interelection decisions are subordinate or executory to those arrived at during the election stage, i.e., elections are in a sense controlling

8.2. Or that new decisions during the interelection period are governed by the preceding seven conditions, operating, however, under rather different institutional circumstances

8.3. Or both.

IV

I think it may be laid down dogmatically that no human organization—certainly none with more than a handful of people—has ever met or is ever likely to meet these eight conditions. It is true that the second, third, and sixth conditions are quite precisely met in some organizations, although in the United States corrupt practices sometimes nullify even these; the others are, at best, only crudely approximated.

As to the first, evidently in all human organizations there are significant variations in participation in political decisions—variations which in the United States appear to be functionally related to such variables as degree of concern or involvement, skill, access, socioeconomic status, education, residence, age, ethnic and religious identifications, and some little understood personality characteristics. As is well known, in national elections on the average something like half of all adults in the United States go to the polls; only a quarter do anything more than vote: write to their congressmen, for example, or contribute to campaigns, or attempt to persuade others to adopt their political views.[6] In the 1952 election, of one nationwide sample only 11 per cent helped the political parties financially, attended party gatherings, or worked for one of the parties or candidates; only 27 per cent talked to other people to try to show them why they should vote for one of the parties or candidates.[7] The effective political elites, then, operate within limits often vague and broad, although occasionally narrow and well defined, set by their expectations as to the reactions of the group of politically active citizens who go to the polls. Other organizations, such as trade-unions, where political equality is prescribed in the formal charter, operate in much the same way, although the elites and the politically active members are often even a smaller proportion of the total.[8]

In no organization of which I have any knowledge does the fourth condition exist. Perhaps the condition is most closely approximated in very small groups. Certainly in all large groups for which we have any data, control over communication is so unevenly distributed that some individuals possess considerably more influence over the designation of the alternatives scheduled for voting than do others. I do not know how to quantify this control, but if it could be quantified I suppose that it would be no exaggeration to say that Mr. Henry Luce has a

6. For example, see Julian L. Woodward and Elmo Roper, "Political Activity of American Citizens," *American Political Science Review*, December, 1950.

7. Angus Campbell, Gerald Gurin, and Warren E. Miller, *The Voter Decides* (Evanston: Row, Peterson & Co., 1954), p. 30, Table 3.1.

8. S. M. Lipset, "The Political Process in Trade Unions: A Theoretical Statement," in *Freedom and Control in Modern Society*, ed. M. Berger, T. Abel, and C. H. Page (New York: D. Van Nostrand Co., Inc., 1954). Joseph Goldstein, *The Government of British Trade Unions: A Study of Apathy and the Democratic Process in the Transport and General Workers Union* (London: Allen & Unwin, 1952). Bernard Barber, "Participation and Mass Apathy in Associations," *Studies in Leadership*, ed. A. W. Gouldner (New York: Harper & Bros., 1950).

thousand or ten thousand times greater control over the alternatives scheduled for debate and tentative decision at a national election than I do. Although we have here a formidable problem that so far as I know has never been adequately analyzed, it is a reasonable preliminary hypothesis that the number of individuals who exercise significant control over the alternatives scheduled is, in most organizations, only a tiny fraction of the total membership. This seems to be the case even in the most democratic organizations if the membership is at all large.

Much the same remarks apply to the fifth condition. The gap in information between the political elites and the active members—not to say the inactive members—no doubt is almost always great. In recent times the gap has been further widened in national governments by growing technical complexities and the rapid spread of security regulations. As every student of bureaucracy knows, the seventh condition is the source of serious difficulties; however, the extent to which this condition is achieved is perhaps the most puzzling of all to measure objectively.

If elections, like the market, were continuous, then we should have no need of the eighth condition. But of course elections are only periodic. It is sometimes suggested that the interelection pressures on decision processes are a kind of election, but this is at best only a deceptive metaphor. If elections with their elaborate machinery, prescribed legal codes, and judicially enforceable opportunities do not in fact maximize political equality and popular sovereignty for the reasons just outlined (as well as many others), then I do not think it can be seriously argued that the interelection process maximizes these goals to anywhere near the same degree.

Because human organizations rarely and perhaps never reach the limit set by these eight conditions, it is necessary to interpret each of the conditions as one end of a continuum or scale along which any given organization might be measured. Unfortunately there is at present no known way of assigning meaningful weights to the eight conditions. However, even without weights, if the eight scales could each be metricized,[9] it would be possible and perhaps useful to establish some

9. This question is discussed briefly in Appendix B to this chapter.

arbitrary but not meaningless classes of which the upper chunk might be called "polyarchies."[10]

It is perfectly evident, however, that what has just been described is no more than a program, for nothing like it has, I think, ever been attempted. I shall simply set down here, therefore, the following observations. Organizations do in fact differ markedly in the extent to which they approach the limits set by these eight conditions. Furthermore, "polyarchies" include a variety of organizations which Western political scientists would ordinarily call democratic, including certain aspects of the governments of nation states such as the United States, Great Britain, the Dominions (South Africa possibly excepted), the Scandinavian countries, Mexico, Italy, and France; states and provinces, such as the states of this country and the provinces of Canada; numerous cities and towns; some trade-unions; numerous associations such as Parent-Teachers' Associations, chapters of the League of Women Voters, and some religious groups; and some primitive societies. Thus it follows that the number of polyarchies is large. (The number of egalitarian polyarchies is probably relatively small or perhaps none exist at all.) The number of polyarchies must run well over a hundred and probably well over a thousand. Of this number, however, only a tiny handful has been exhaustively studied by political scientists, and these have been the most difficult of all, the governments of national states, and in a few instances the smaller governmental units.

Some will be quick to insist that the differences among particular types of polyarchies, e.g., between nation states and trade-unions, are so great that it is not likely to be useful to include them in the same class. I do not think we have nearly enough evidence for such a conclusion. At any rate, given such a large number of cases to study, in principle it should be possible to answer the question: What are the necessary and sufficient conditions for polyarchies to exist?

Thus we see that the first method of constructing a theory of democracy, the method of maximization described in chapter 1, merges here with what I have called the descriptive method. We started by

10. Appendix D to this chapter suggests a possible classification scheme.

searching for the conditions that would be necessary and sufficient in the real world in order to maximize so far as may be possible popular sovereignty and political equality. We found that we could answer this question by measuring the extent to which the Rule is employed in an organization. But in order to measure the extent to which the Rule is employed, we had to lay down eight more or less observable conditions. These we interpreted first as limits, which we saw to be unattained in the real world and quite probably unattainable; and then we reinterpreted them as ends of eight continua or scales which, it was suggested, might be used in measurements. Now our question must be rephrased as follows: What are the necessary and sufficient conditions in the real world for the existence of these eight conditions, to at least the minimum degree we have agreed to call polyarchy? In order to answer the question, it would be necessary to classify and study a considerable number of real world organizations. Thus we close the circle between the method of maximization and the descriptive method.

V

To carry out this program rigorously is a task far beyond the scope of these essays and quite possibly beyond the scope of political science at the present time. However we can set down some hypotheses for which considerable evidence exists.

To begin with, each of the eight conditions can be formulated as a rule or, if you prefer, a norm. For example, from the first condition we can derive a norm to the effect that every member ought to have an opportunity to express his preferences. It would seem truistic that if all the members of an organization rejected the norms prescribing the eight conditions, then the conditions would not exist; or alternatively, the extent to which polyarchy exists must be related to the extent to which the norms are accepted as desirable. If we are willing to assume that the extent of agreement (consensus) on the eight basic norms is measurable, then we can formulate the following hypotheses, which have been commonplace in the literature of political science:

1. Each of the conditions of polyarchy increases with the extent of agreement (or consensus) on the relevant norm.

2. Polyarchy is a function of consensus on the eight norms, other things remaining the same.[11]

Unfortunately for the simplicity of the hypotheses, consensus possesses at least three dimensions: the number of individuals who agree, the intensity or depth of their belief, and the extent to which overt activity conforms with belief. Nevertheless, it is worth setting out explicitly what may at first sight seem trivial if not purely definitional, for it is a curious and possibly significant fact that despite the hoary respectability of the hypotheses among political scientists, so far as I know, no one has assembled the empirical data necessary for even a preliminary confirmation of their validity. We do have a reassuring amount of quite indirect evidence that agreement on the eight norms is less in, say, Germany than in England, but it seems to me highly arbitrary to leave our crucial hypotheses in such a careless state.

The extent of agreement, in turn, must be functionally dependent upon the extent to which the various processes for social training are employed on behalf of the norms by the family, schools, churches, clubs, literature, newspapers, and the like. Again, if it were possible to measure the extent to which these processes are used, our hypotheses could be stated as:

3. The extent of agreement (consensus) on each of the eight norms increases with the extent of social training in the norm.

4. Consensus is therefore a function of the total social training in all the norms.

It also follows from the preceding hypotheses that:

5. Polyarchy is a function of the total social training in all the norms.[12] As before, the variable "training" is a highly complex one. At a minimum one would need to distinguish favorable or reinforcing, compatible (or neutral), and negative training. It is reasonable to suppose that these three kinds of training operate on members of most if not all polyarchal organizations and perhaps on members of many hier-

11. Appendix E to this chapter raises some questions about treating polyarchy as positive and increasing with both consensus and political activity.

12. For a "Summary of the hypothetical functions relating polyarchy to its preconditions" see Appendix C to this chapter.

archical organizations as well. But very little reliable knowledge seems to exist on this question.[13]

In principle we need not end the chain of relationships with training. Why, one might ask, do some social organizations engage in extensive training in the norms and others in little or none? The answer is apparently lost in the complexities of historical accident, but a useful subsidiary hypothesis suggests itself, namely, that the extent to which training is given in these norms is not independent of the extent of agreement that exists on choices among policy alternatives.[14] It is reasonable to suppose that the less the agreement on policy choices, the more difficult it will be in any organization to train members in the eight norms. For then, although the operation of the rules may confer benefits on some members, it will impose severe restraints on others. If the results are severe for relatively large numbers, then it is reasonable to suppose that those who suffer from the operation of the rules will oppose them and hence resist training in them. Thus:

6. Social training in the eight norms increases with the extent of consensus or agreement on choices among policy alternatives.

From 5 and 6 it follows that:

7. One or more of the conditions of polyarchy increases with consensus on policy alternatives.

Hypothesis 6 suggests, moreover, that the reverse of Hypothesis 4 is also valid. We would expect that the extent to which social training in the norms is indulged in is itself dependent upon the amount of agreement that already exists on the norms. The more disagreement there is about the norms, the more likely it is that some of the means of

13. No doubt the pioneer work here is Plato's *Republic*. In modern times the most ambitious attempt to examine this problem seems to have been that inspired by Charles Merriam, including his own *The Making of Citizens* (Chicago: University of Chicago Press, 1931). Cf. also Elizabeth A. Weber, *The Duk-Duks, Primitive and Historic Types of Citizenship* (Chicago: University of Chicago Press, 1929).

14. A highly interesting, factual, and speculative examination of consensus on issues as revealed in Elmira, New York, is contained in B. R. Berelson, Paul F. Lazarsfeld, and William N. McPhee, *Voting* (Chicago: University of Chicago Press, 1954), chap. ix. Indeed, the entire volume is relevant to the empirical study of polyarchy.

social training—the family and the school in particular—will train some individuals in conflicting norms. The relationship between social training and consensus is thus a perfect instance of the hen-and-egg problem. Hence:

8. The extent of social training in one of the eight norms also increases with the extent of agreement on it.

A relationship that gives rise to occasional confusion is that between polyarchy and social diversity. One often hears it said that "democracy requires diversity of opinion." Certainly it is true that diversity of opinion is a fact of human society; in no known society do all members agree on all policies all the time, and this fact makes it necessary that all social organizations possess some means, however primitive, for settling conflicts over goals. The proposition might even be maintained that because some conflict over goals is inevitable in human organizations, polyarchies are necessary to maximize human welfare—if that term could be suitably defined. In the opinion of many people, diversity, up to some ill-defined point, has other values—aesthetic, emotional, and intellectual. It may also be true, as Mill contended, that some diversity of opinion is a necessary condition for rational calculation about alternative policies. But each of these propositions is quite different from the assertion that diversity of opinion, or conflict over goals, is a necessary condition for polyarchy.[15] For if our argument so far is correct, then it cannot be altogether true that polyarchy requires disagreement either about the validity of the eight basic norms or about particular public policies. At any rate, the relationship is not a simple one.

In the United States we have glorified a historic inevitability as a virtue. (I hope that we shall continue to do so.) Yet the glorification of diversity should not be permitted to confuse us about important social relationships. Is there, then, nothing in our traditional viewpoint? What of Madison's often-repeated hypothesis in *The Federalist*, No. 10?

15. The proposition is valid, of course, in the following trivial sense. Human society is necessary for polyarchy. A fundamental characteristic of human societies is conflict over goals. *Ergo....*

Extend the sphere, and you take in a greater variety of parties and interests; you make it less probable that a majority of the whole will have a common motive to invade the rights of other citizens; or if such a common motive exists, it will be more difficult for all who feel it to discover their own strength, and to act in unison with each other.

In order to grapple with this question of the relationship, if any, between diversity and democracy, we need to distinguish carefully between two rather different categories—or, as I prefer to think of them —continua.

(*a*) One is the continuum from agreement to disagreement over goals. Here we must further distinguish between agreement on political goals and on non-political goals. A political goal is any objective which individuals seek to forward or inhibit by means of government action.[16] In Hypotheses 1 to 5 we have, in effect, distinguished two kinds of political goals: the goals embodied in the eight basic norms and policy goals. The argument so far is that polyarchy requires a relatively high agreement on both kinds of political goals.

(*b*) The other is a continuum from autonomy to control. A group is autonomous to the extent that its policies are not controlled by individuals outside the group.

Madison's argument in effect states that a relatively high degree of group autonomy combined with a relatively high degree of disagreement over goals will act as an important limitation on the capacity of any putative majority to control government policy. But if we are concerned, as we are in this essay, with the conditions under which the existence of the Rule may be maximized, we do not find this a very happy answer. Hence we need to reconstruct Madison's argument; and while he would have put the following reconstruction with an elegance, force, and precision that are beyond my powers, I do not believe that he would have disagreed with the analysis.

Let us imagine two groups of individuals. Group A prefers policy x

16. I do not want to pursue an endless regression in definitions. In these essays the meaning of "government" can either be accepted as intuitively more or less clear or the following definition can be used, despite its limitations: Government is the group of individuals with a sufficient monopoly of control to enforce orderly settlements of disputes.

to policy y and the other prefers y to x. Now, remembering that the complete social autonomy of a group is (definitionally) identical with the complete absence of control by any outside individuals or groups, if Group A and Group B are completely autonomous with respect to one another on all policies, then no governmental relation exists between them, and hence they cannot be members of the same polyarchy. Given these extreme conditions, no political question will arise because of their disagreement.[17] Conversely, if the members of Groups A and B are autonomous on no choices, including x and y, then, in principle, polyarchy is possible among them, i.e., the Rule may be applied to resolve the question of x or y. Aside from other difficulties that may be imagined, if there is no autonomy and if the disagreement over x and y is very strong—as, for example, in such a question as slavery which goes to the very essentials of social structure and ideology—then, as has been suggested in connection with Hypothesis 4, agreement on and training in the eight basic norms necessary to polyarchy will probably be reduced, perhaps drastically. That is, disagreement plus no autonomy undermines polyarchy.

If, however, the two groups are autonomous with respect to one another, at least on the choice between x and y, then the decision is no longer a political one for which the machinery of polyarchy needs to be employed. It becomes, like religious toleration, a non-political question, and different choices may be compatible with a high degree of agreement on and training in the basic norms necessary for polyarchy. Hence we formulate the following hypothesis:

Beyond some point, the sharper the disagreement over policies within a social organization, and the larger the proportion of individuals involved in the disagreement, the greater the amount of social autonomy required for polyarchy to exist at any given level.

Now the extent of agreement cannot be considered entirely independently of the extent of political activity in an organization. The extent to which some of the conditions for polyarchy—1, 4, and 5—are met is also a measure of the political activity of members, that is, the extent to which they vote in elections and primaries, participate in

17. Under the conditions stated even war is ruled out.

campaigns, and seek and disseminate information and propaganda. Thus by definition:

9. Polyarchy is a function of the political activity of the members.[18]

A good deal is now known about the variables with which political activity is associated; indeed, the next decade should produce a rather precise set of propositions about these relationships. At present we know that political activity, at least in the United States, is positively associated to a significant extent with such variables as income, socio-economic status, and education, and that it is also related in complex ways with belief systems, expectations, and personality structures. We now know that members of the ignorant and unpropertied masses which Madison and his colleagues so much feared are considerably less active politically than the educated and well-to-do. By their propensity for political passivity the poor and uneducated disfranchise themselves.[19] Since they also have less access than the wealthy to the organizational, financial, and propaganda resources that weigh so heavily in campaigns, elections, legislative, and executive decisions, anything like equal control over government policy is triply barred to the members of Madison's unpropertied masses. They are barred by their relatively greater inactivity, by their relatively limited access to resources, and by Madison's nicely contrived system of constitutional checks.

VI

These, then, are some of the relationships that we political scientists need to explore with the aid of our colleagues in other social sciences. That they are only a few of the crucial relationships is hardly contestable. For example, a relationship, even if a complex one, undoubtedly exists between the extent of political equality possible in a society and the distribution of income, wealth, status, and control over organizational resources. Moreover, it is increasingly likely that

18. For an important complexity in this hypothetical function, see Appendix E to this chapter, "A note on the relation between agreement and political activity."

19. Cf. especially B. R. Berelson, P. F. Lazarsfeld, and W. N. McPhee, *op. cit.*; S. M. Lipset *et al.*, "The Psychology of Voting: An Analysis of Political Behavior, *Handbook of Social Psychology* (Cambridge: Addison-Wesley, 1954).

some relationship exists between the extent of polyarchy and the personality structures of the members of an organization; we now speak of authoritarian and democratic personality types, even if our knowledge of these hypothetical types and their actual distribution in different societies is still highly fragmentary. It is too early to say, I think, that a high correlation has been established between polyarchy and the relative presence or absence of particular personality types; but certainly the efficacy of social training in the basic norms, mentioned above, must partly depend upon the deepest predispositions of the individual.

Because concern with the social prerequisites of different political orders is as old as political speculation, no claim can be made for the novelty of the hypotheses in this chapter. I have simply set forth, sometimes more rigorously than is customary, a body of propositions hinted at, suggested by, inferred from, and often enough openly stated by various political scientists from Socrates to the present. Nevertheless, it may be useful to distinguish this approach, if only in degree, from the Madisonian and populistic.

Madison's compromise between the power of majorities and the power of minorities rested in large part, although not wholly, upon the existence of constitutional restraints upon majority action. As distinguished from Madisonianism, the theory of polyarchy focuses primarily not on the constitutional prerequisites but on the social prerequisites for a democratic order. The difference is one of degree: Madison, as we saw, was not indifferent to the necessary social conditions for his non-tyrannical republic. But surely it is not unfair to say that his primary concern was with prescribed constitutional controls rather than with the operating social controls, with constitutional checks and balances rather than with social checks and balances. After all, the Constitutional Convention had to design a constitution; it could not design a society. The men at the Convention took human nature and social structure largely for granted; their job, as they interpreted it, was to create a constitution most fully consonant both with human nature and social structure and with the goal of a republic respectful of natural rights, particularly the natural rights of the well-born and the few.

Yet the bent given to American thought by the Constitutional Convention and the subsequent apotheosis of its product have, I believe, hindered realistic and precise thinking about the requirements of democracy. It is significant that right up until Fort Sumter fell, the dispute between North and South was, with only a few important exceptions, cast almost entirely in the language of constitutional law. The tragedy of the Dred Scott decision was not so much its outcome as the state of mind it bespoke.

Because we are taught to believe in the necessity of constitutional checks and balances, we place little faith in social checks and balances. We admire the efficacy of constitutional separation of powers in curbing majorities and minorities, but we often ignore the importance of the restraits imposed by social separation of powers. Yet if the theory of polyarchy is roughly sound, it follows that in the absence of certain social prerequisites, no constitutional arrangements can produce a non-tyrannical republic. The history of numerous Latin-American states is, I think, sufficient evidence. Conversely, an increase in the extent to which one of the social prerequisites is present may be far more important in strengthening democracy than any particular constitutional design. Whether we are concerned with tyranny by a minority or tyranny by a majority, the theory of polyarchy suggests that the first and crucial variables to which political scientists must direct their attention are social and not constitutional.

Populistic theory as it was outlined in the last chapter was found to be formal and axiomatic but lacking in information about the real world. To say that perfect attainment of political equality and popular sovereignty is, by definition of terms, consistent only with the majority principle is not to enunciate a wholly useless proposition, but neither is it very helpful. For what we desperately want to know (if we are concerned with political equality) is what we may do to maximize it in some actual situation, given existing conditions.

If we wish to turn our attention to the chaos of the real world without getting totally lost in meaningless facts and trivial empiricism we need theory to help us order the incredible and baffling array of events. The theory of polyarchy, an inadequate, incomplete, primitive ordering of the common store of knowledge about democracy, is formulated in the conviction that somewhere between chaos and tautology we shall be able sometime to construct a satisfactory theory about political equality.

APPENDIX TO CHAPTER 3

A. *The definitional characteristics of polyarchy*

Polyarchy is defined loosely as a political system in which the following conditions exist to a relatively high degree:

During the voting period:

1. Every member of the organization performs the acts we assume to constitute an expression of preference among the scheduled alternatives, e.g., voting.

2. In tabulating these expressions (votes), the weight assigned to the choice of each individual is identical.

3. The alternative with the greatest number of votes is declared the winning choice.

During the prevoting period:

4. Any member who perceives a set of alternatives, at least one of which he regards as preferable to any of the alternatives presently scheduled, can insert his preferred alternative(s) among those scheduled for voting.

5. All individuals possess identical information about the alternatives.

During the postvoting period:

6. Alternatives (leaders or policies) with the greatest number of votes displace any alternatives (leaders or policies) with fewer votes.

7. The orders of elected officials are executed.

During the interelection stage:

8.1. Either all interelection decisions are subordinate or executory to those arrived at during the election stage, i.e., elections are in a sense controlling

8.2. Or new decisions during the interelection period are governed by the preceding seven conditions, operating, however, under rather different institutional circumstances

8.3. Or both.

B. *The measurement of polyarchy*

In order to arrive at a set of scales with which to measure polyarchy quantitatively, each of these conditions may be considered as designating certain actions the frequency of which can, in principle, be determined. If frequencies can be determined then we may convert the conditions either into statements about past frequencies, say, along a scale from 0 to 100, or about expected future frequencies, that is, probabilities ranged along a scale from 0 to 1.

Thus the first condition can be converted into the statement that polyarchy is a function of the following variable: The fraction of the total membership who perform (or alternatively, the probability that any randomly selected member will perform) the act we assume to constitute an expression of preference among the scheduled alternatives. (This fraction can be designated as P_1.) It happens, however, that the first condition is most amenable to this treatment, for excellent data exist in most organizations on the extent of participation in voting, the act which ordinarily, no doubt, would be used as the index of preference. Unfortunately, however, as we proceed down the list a number of difficulties present themselves. For some conditions our knowledge is not, as in the case of elections, already in quantitative form nor is it likely to be; we have no frequency tables, for example, for Condition 7, and it is clear that formidable problems would arise in the attempt to determine such frequencies. In these cases frequencies or probabilities might have to be assigned by the observer in an intuitive and rather arbitrary way. Moreover, some of the conditions are complex ones and would be meaningless if their ordering were to ignore these complexities. For example, in Condition 2 we would want to take into account more than the frequency with which, or the probability that, some votes or voters will be weighted more than others. Until recently in Great Britain, about 375,000 people had an extra vote (either because they held a university degree or because they had business premises in a constituency different from their residence). Hence Condition 2 was certainly violated at every election; but it was a relatively minor violation if we consider the magnitude of the electorate, for in 1945 those with extra votes were only about 1.2 per cent of the total electorate. What this suggests, however, is that we would want a measure of Condition 2 to take into account both the proportion of votes or voters weighted excessively and the comparative weights. It might be possible to design a scale to take these factors into account, though it is worth mentioning that out of a half-dozen or so which initially seemed to me promising, all proved to be defective in one way or another. The best might be something like the following:

$$P_2 = 1 - \frac{\sum_{i=1}^{K} |\overline{W} - W_i| N_i}{\sum_{i=1}^{K} W_i N_i},$$

where W is the weight of the vote, N is the number of citizens or voters with that particular vote, and $\overline{W}$ is the mean weighted vote. This formula would give values approaching 0 as the magnitude of the deviations increased and equaling 1 in the case where all citizens had votes of equal weight. In the British case, mentioned above, the result would be about 0.98.

Conditions 4 and 5 are perhaps even more formidable, for while it is easy enough to detect the gross presence or absence of these conditions, to order the different possible, and indeed probable, states of affairs along the continuum will present numerous problems; needless to say, to impose a metrical scale on any such ordering would be even more difficult—if not, indeed, ludicrous.

C. *Summary of the hypothetical functions relating polyarchy and its preconditions*

The specific shape of the following functions is not known, except that the dependent variable is assumed to be a positive and increasing function of the independent variable when all other factors are fixed. Hence, let $\uparrow$ signify this relation.

(1) $P_1 \uparrow C_1$ when P_1 is one of the definitional characteristics of polyarchy and C_1 is the consensus on the relevant norm.

$$P_2 \uparrow C_2$$
$$. . . . .$$
$$P_8 \uparrow C_8$$

(2) $P \uparrow (C_1, C_2 \ldots C_8, X)$, where X is all other preconditions on which polyarchy is dependent.

(3) $C_1 \uparrow S_1$, where S_1 is social training in that norm.

$$C_2 \uparrow S_2$$
$$. . . . .$$
$$C_8 \uparrow S_8$$

(4) $C \uparrow (S_1, S_2 \ldots S_8, X)$

(5) $P_1 \uparrow S_1$, etc.,

$$\text{and } P \uparrow (S, X)$$

(6) $S \uparrow Ca$, where Ca is consensus on policy alternatives.

(7) $P \uparrow Ca$

(8) $S_1 \uparrow (Ca, C_1)$

$$S_2 \uparrow (Ca, C_2)$$
$$. . . . .$$
$$S_8 \uparrow (Ca, C_8)$$
$$\text{and}$$
$$S \uparrow (Ca, C_1, C_2 \ldots C_8)$$

(9) $P\uparrow(A, X)$, where A is political activity.

(10) $P\uparrow(Ca, C_{1-8}, S, A, X)$

D. A possible classification of polyarchies

1. Polyarchies are defined as: organizations in which all eight conditions are scaled at values equal to or greater than 0.5.

1.1. Egalitarian polyarchies are defined as: polyarchies in which all eight conditions are scaled at values equal to or greater than 0.75.

1.2. Non-egalitarian polyarchies are defined as all other polyarchies.

2. Hierarchies are defined as: organizations in which all eight conditions are scaled at values less than 0.5.

2.1. Oligarchies are defined as: hierarchies in which some conditions are scaled at values equal to or greater than 0.25.

2.2. Dictatorships are defined as: hierarchies in which no conditions are scaled at values equal to 0.25.

3. Mixed polities are defined as: the residual, i.e., organizations in which at least one condition is scaled at a value greater than or equal to 0.5, and at least one at a value less than 0.5.

E. A note on the relationship between agreement and political activity

So far as I am aware, very little reliable knowledge exists on the relationship between agreement and political activity and therefore on the relationship of the variables of hypotheses (2), (7), and (10) above. Francis Wilson has argued, in effect, that political activity tends to be inversely related to agreement on policy alternatives.[20] Symbolically:

(11) $A\uparrow-Ca$

From which it would follow, if our hypothesis (9) is correct, that

(12) $P\uparrow-Ca$

But clearly (7) and (12) cannot be true, for polyarchy cannot both increase and decrease with the extent of consensus over the total range.

V. O. Key has, I think, demonstrated that Wilson's hypothesis is not supported by such empirical evidence as we now have; and that, indeed, the converse might be maintained with as much or better reason. Thus we cannot reasonably argue that consensus is less in New Zealand, where 90 per cent of the adult population frequently goes to the polls in national elections, than in the United States, where 50–60 per cent vote.

Nevertheless, it is not unreasonable to suppose that within a given nation or other social organization there is over time some discernible association between the extent of political activity and the extent of disagreement on

20. "The Inactive Electorate and Social Revolution," *Southwestern Political Science Quarterly*, XVI, No. 4 (1936), 73–84, cited in V. O. Key, *Politics and Pressure Groups* (3d ed.; New York: Thomas Y. Crowell, 1952), p. 58.

policy alternatives. In a hypothetical situation where only two alternatives are perceived the simplest case would be one like the following:

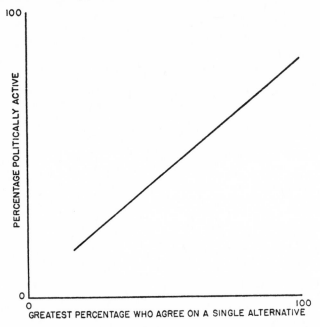

Of course the straight line is arbitrary; so long as the slope of the curve is always positive, any increase in consensus or any increase in political activity must be associated with an increase in polyarchy. Now, it is reasonable to suppose that where consensus is very low, that is, where there is little agreement on any alternative, and hence great difficulty in achieving any alternative, apathy may result. Likewise, it is reasonable to suppose that where consensus is very high, many individuals will feel little need to vote or otherwise to influence political decisions. If these suppositions were correct, then we would expect, up to some point, activity to rise with increasing agreement and thereafter to decline, as in the following diagram.

From A to B no problem arises. From B to C, however, political activity decreases as agreement on policy increases. But decreasing political activity means that the values of P_1, P_4, and P_5 would decline, i.e., polyarchy would decrease. Yet according to hypothesis (7) polyarchy would tend to increase.

If we had sufficient data the contradiction could probably be resolved. In the first place, we could then specify the domains within which the various functions apply. In the second place, we could introduce the time factor, which is ignored in the hypotheses but is undoubtedly of crucial importance. Thus an increase or decrease in agreement may only slowly show up in increased or decreased social training, whereas it may show up in political activity much more quickly. Finally, we could determine whether the relationships are reversible; they need not be. An increase in agreement may not decrease political activity by as large an amount as an equivalent decrease in agreement will increase it. Here the problems of empirical knowledge are formidable and quite possibly insoluble in any except very loose form.

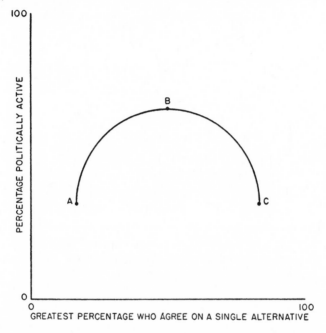

The same difficulties apply to the relationship between polyarchy, political activity, and consensus on the basic norms. But here we may encounter an added problem, for current evidence suggests that in the United States the lower one's socioeconomic class, the more authoritarian one's predispositions and the less active politically one is likely to be. Thus if an increase in political activity brings the authoritarian-minded into the political arena, consensus on the basic norms among the politically active certainly must be declining. To the extent that consensus declines, we would expect from hypothesis (1) that, after some lag, polyarchy would also decline.

In the light of all this we cannot assume that an increase in political activity is always associated with an increase in polyarchy, as indicated in hypothesis (9). The relationship is evidently a highly complex one; it needs a great deal more careful research and theory construction.

CHAPTER 4

Equality
Diversity
and Intensity

I

Is there no clear-cut solution to the problem Madison wrestled with and for which he designed his compromise? Is it possible to construct a system for arriving at decisions that is compatible with the idea of political equality and at the same time protects the rights of minorities? Madison's own solution, as we saw, was shot through with assumptions and arguments that do not stand up under criticism. In what I chose to call populistic theory—starting from the premises of popular sovereignty and political equality—we deduced by strict logic that the only procedural rule compatible with these two goals is the majority principle. By making "most preferred" equivalent to "preferred by the most" we deliberately bypassed a crucial problem: What if the minority prefers its alternative much more passionately than the majority prefers a contrary alternative? Does the majority principle still make sense?

This is the problem of intensity. And as one can readily see, intensity is almost a modern psychological version of natural rights. For just as Madison believed that government should be constructed so as to prevent majorities from invading the natural rights of minorities, so a modern Madison might argue that government should be designed to inhibit a relatively apathetic majority from cramming its policy down the throats of a relatively intense minority.

II

Unfortunately, intensity is not easy to define. As a preliminary definition we might say that it is the degree to which one wants or prefers some alternative.[1] If, however, we wish to restrict ourselves to what we can observe, what shall we agree to mean by saying that A prefers x to y? If A is Jones, x "the company of blondes," and y "the company of brunettes," then we must mean that when Jones has an opportunity to choose, he chooses the company of blondes rather than brunettes. Or at a minimum, some part of his observed behavior—in this case, perhaps, what Jones tells us about himself—permits us to predict that he will choose blondes rather than brunettes.

Note that we cannot say how much he prefers blondes to brunettes. Jones himself has no need to know how much he prefers blondes to brunettes; yet the basic fact that we cannot measure the intensity of his preferences raises some interesting and indeed serious problems for democratic theory. For if we cannot measure how much Jones prefers blondes to brunettes, or how much Smith prefers brunettes to blondes, what can we possibly mean when we say that Jones prefers blondes to brunettes more than Smith prefers brunettes to blondes? Surprising as it may seem, in the general case (if not in this specific one), the question is highly troublesome.[2] For how can we ever know that some minority prefers its alternative more than the majority? Is the antithesis between an intense minority and an apathetic majority meaningless?

It may be argued that even if the antithesis is not meaningless, it is irrelevant. Yet there are two reasons why it would be important to estimate intensities—why one may want to know whether an alterna-

1. The reader will understand that wanting an alternative includes wanting not to have some specified alternative. That is, wanting not to be forced to take alternative x is to want alternative "not-x." "Want" and "prefer" are used interchangeably in the discussion that follows.

2. Notice that we are excluding here two other questions of less relevance to democratic theory:
   (1) If A and B both prefer x to y, does A prefer x to y more than B prefers x to y?
   (2) If A prefers x to y and B prefers p to q, does A prefer x to y more than B prefers p to q?

A moment's reflection will, I think, show why these questions are not of great relevance to democratic theory.

tive is only slightly preferred by a majority and intensely distasteful to some minority.

The first reason is essentially ethical in character, and not everyone will agree that it is important. Suppose that A prefers x to y, B prefers y to x, and the choice of one excludes the other. Many of us would like to know whether A prefers x to y more than B prefers y to x. All other things being the same, many of us would want A to have his alternative if his preference were considerably more intense. Of course all other things frequently are not the same, and then we may want to disregard intensities. But if the outcome is otherwise a matter of indifference, it might seem fair to establish the rule that the individual with the more intense preference should get his way.

If a collective decision is involved, one that requires voting, would it be possible to construct rules so that an apathetic majority only slightly preferring its alternative could not override a minority strongly preferring its alternative? I shall not try to prove that such rules would be desirable; but if they could be designed, evidently they would answer a problem that, in one way or another, has frequently disturbed democratic theorists, particularly in the United States. The modern invocation of Calhoun's idea of "concurrent majorities" is perhaps an effort to prove the need for such rules and the manner in which they might be designed.

The second reason why the comparison of intensities of preference is important arises from a desire to predict the stability of a democratic system and perhaps even to design rules to guarantee its stability. As an illustration let us assume a simple bipolar situation where citizens must choose or reject some alternative. Let us suppose further that we have carefully polled samples of citizens in order to determine, after excluding those who are indifferent or have no opinion, the proportions who are for and against the policy. Each of these major groups is, in turn, subdivided into those strongly, moderately, or slightly for or against. We can now imagine six different types of distribution.

First, opinion may be overwhelmingly for (or against) the policy, with the greatest number feeling a strong preference, as in Figure 2. Or opinion may be overwhelmingly for (or against) the alternative, with the greatest number only slightly for (against) it, as in Figure 3. Third, opinion may be more or less evenly split for and against it but with the preponderant numbers only slightly preferring their alternative, as in Figures 4 and 5.

Now in a polyarchal social organization that employs the Rule during the process of choosing policy, none of these distributions raises

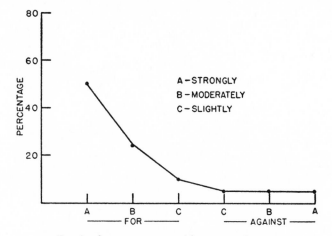

F*ig.* 2.—Strong consensus with strong preferences

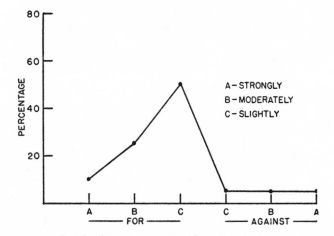

F*ig.* 3.—Strong consensus with weak preferences

any serious problems. In so far as we are concerned with intensities, application of the Rule is not ethically repugnant[3] or is it likely to produce instability.

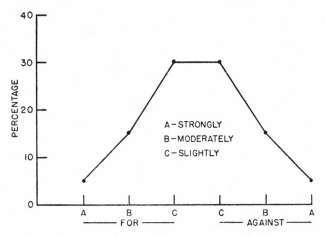

FIG. 4.—Moderate disagreement: symmetrical

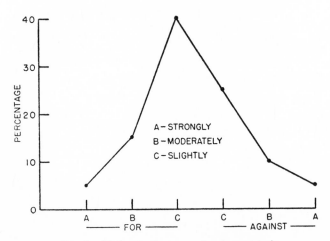

FIG. 5.—Moderate disagreement: asymmetrical

3. In the limited sense of the problem under consideration here. That is, in these instances the majority, where one exists, contains at least as many individuals who are strongly for or against the policy as does the minority.

Although the data are very fragmentary indeed, it is a reasonable hypothesis that opinion on major issues in stable polyarchies tends to vary among these four types. Thus in response to the question "Do you think it would make a good deal of difference to the country whether the Democrats or Republicans win the election . . . or that it won't make much difference which side wins?" among a national

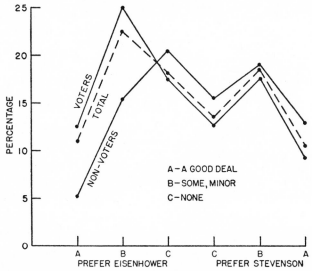

Source: Angus Campbell, Gerald Gurin, and Warren E. Miller, *The Voter Decides*, p. 38, Table 3.9. The response "It depends" was not more than 1 per cent in any category. "Don't know or not ascertained" varied from 4-11 per cent. Neither is included in Fig. 6.

Fig. 6.—Preferences of voters in the 1952 presidential election. Responses to the question, "Do you think it would make a good deal of difference to the country whether the Democrats or Republicans win the elections . . . or that it won't make much difference which side wins?"

sample interviewed during the seven weeks before the 1952 election, only about a fifth thought it would make a good deal of difference to the country, whereas nearly a third thought it would make no difference. The responses are distributed rather like our hypothetical distribution in Figure 5. That is, the election of 1952 was evidently a case of moderate, asymmetrical disagreement (see Fig. 6). In this poll as in many others, however, the phrasing of the question makes a vast amount of difference. Thus when the question was asked "Would you say you personally care a good deal which party wins the presidential election this fall, or that you don't care very much which party wins?" the distribution changes (see Fig. 7). Slightly more than a quarter say they "care very much" and only about one-eighth say that they "don't care at all." However, the moderates who "care somewhat" (39 per cent) together with the relatively indifferent who do not care very much or not at all still constitute over two-thirds of the total. It seems likely

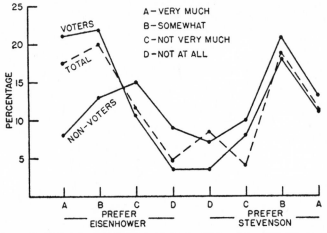

Source: Campbell et al, *op. cit.* Responses tabulated as "It depends" and "Don't know or not ascertained" account for less than 5 per cent in all three categories and were not included in Fig. 7.

FIG. 7.—Preferences of voters in the 1952 presidential election. "Would you say you personally care a good deal which party wins the presidential election this fall, or that you don't care very much which party wins?"

that the first question would provide a more reliable basis for predicting possible postelection discontent and resistance than the second, but in either case as the proportion at the extremes increased we should expect that a peaceful acceptance of the election outcome would become less and less likely.

That is, let us suppose that each side comes to regard the victory of the other as a fundamental threat to some very highly ranked values. In the decade before the American Civil War the struggle over the disposition of the western lands became increasingly intense; while at the beginning of that fateful decade compromise solutions were still possible, by its end no acceptable compromises could be discovered. For it had become more and more clear to southern leaders that if slavery were prohibited in the territories and these vast areas came into the Union as free states, then in time the free states would be able to control public policy and even to alter the Constitution itself. To be sure, many later writers have concluded that the institution of slavery would have been uneconomic in the western territories and therefore could not have survived there or perhaps even in the South. All that is relevant here, however, is that many people in the North evidently believed that if slavery were permitted in the territories, this would alter the political balance against the free states and ultimately frustrate the rising pressure for free lands. Thus any election interpreted as a clear-cut victory for one side was almost certain to be so intolerable to the other that it would refuse to accept the outcome. We surmise that in 1860 such an election took place. This does not mean that many voters had this issue uppermost in their minds when they went to the polls, for it is entirely possible that the election of 1860 was decided mainly on issues other than slavery and free lands. Nevertheless, the election precipitated a series of decisions, each one of which evidently closed out certain alternatives; by the spring of 1861 the alternatives were rapidly narrowing down to a small number, all of which were intolerable to one of the two sides. Civil war may not have been inevitable. But a stable polyarchy including both North and South had become highly improbable.

Resistance to the operation of majority rule can take several forms, depending upon the relative size of the defeated minority and the victorious majority, their geographical location, their access to resources, their belief systems, and the nature of the issues between them. The Whisky Rebellion was not revolution; it was only resistance to tax collectors. Another possibility is a *coup d'état* or revolutionary seizure of power as in Spain with Franco, in Czechoslovakia with the Communists, or in France with Louis Napoleon. Secession is a third possibility. We might even wish to include overt compliance **and** secret rejection of the legitimacy of the political order as a fourth possibility. In any event, where each side is large and each regards the victory of the other as a fundamental threat to some very highly ranked values, it is reasonable to expect serious difficulties in the continued operation of a polyarchal system.

This case is suggested in Figure 8. Whenever something approximating to this distribution persists, no constitutional machinery is likely to guarantee the application of the Rule. Rejection of the Rule may appear in the shape of a refusal to comply with the law, revolu-

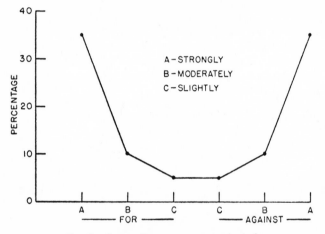

FIG. 8.—Severe disagreement: symmetrical

tion, secession, withdrawal of legitimacy from polyarchal government, or other means. Of this much we can be certain: the system of checks and balances in the Madisonian constitution did not prevent one of the bloodiest civil wars in the history of Western man. None of the numerous constitutional devices suggested at the time proved acceptable, and even in retrospect it is impossible to discover any purely constitutional solution for what was a profoundly rooted social conflict.

Thus if the first four distributions raise no special problems for polyarchies, the distribution in Figure 8 may be said to lie outside its capacities; therefore, it too can be ignored in the discussion that follows. However, let us now distinguish from the distribution in Figure 8 a rather different kind of disagreement, namely, where a large minority has a strong preference for one of two alternatives and the opposing majority has only a slight preference for the other one (see Fig. 9). If there is any case that might be considered the modern analogue to Madison's implicit concept of tyranny, I suppose it is this one. Indeed, it is often held that the various features of the American political system that modify the straightforward operation of majority rule are of particularly crucial importance in resolving situations of this kind.

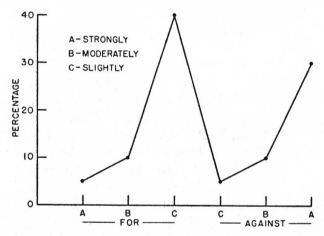

Fɪɢ. 9.—Severe disagreement: asymmetrical

III

I have now suggested two reasons why it would be helpful for the development of democratic theory if we could assume that some means exist for comparing intensities of preference. But do such means exist?

If by "intensity" we mean the sensations of another person, then we are defeated at the outset. It is obvious that we can never directly observe the sensations of another person; whatever we experience directly, or whatever we observe by introspection, are always our own sensations. In no conceivable way, then, can we directly observe and compare the sensate intensities of preference of different individuals. More than that, since we can never directly observe the sensations of others we can never treat sensations as observable variables with which, given a sufficient number of cases, we could correlate changes in facial expression, words, posture, or even the chemistry of the body. We can correlate chemical changes in the body with changes in the words our subject uses about his sensations, but the sensations themselves will always elude us. We can and do postulate that sensations do exist in others, but we cannot directly observe them. In this sense of measuring intensities of feeling or sensation, it is meaningless to say that A prefers x to y more than B prefers y to x.

Yet most of us will continue to make such statements and to believe that they are meaningful. We shall argue whether Ellen really wants her dress more than Peter wants his transformer or Eric his bicycle, and we shall not for a moment doubt that our discussion is meaningful. We shall continue to believe not only that we can guess intelligently but that we must guess intelligently about such things. I think that the core of meaning is to be found in the assumption that the uniformities we observe in human beings must carry over, in part, to the unobservables like feeling and sensation; to assume that sensation is autonomous and not reliably connected with overt behavior seems more arbitrary and less sensible than the alternative postulate. In a sense we are denying that every individual is unique and therefore unknowable; we are assuming that there are uniformities. We assume further that some uniformities in overt behavior are roughly associated with some uniformities in inner states, although we soon discover that a whole lifetime will be insufficient to explore all the subtle relationships between observable behavior and the inner life we postulate in others.

Out of all the kinds of overt behavior we observe, we select some as possible measuring rods. Even when we apply each with great care, in the end we still cannot escape the fact that we do not know whether these measuring rods really measure sensate intensity. However, since we must act somehow, we use these as guesses or postulates. Then we seek to reduce a situation of choice to these postulated measuring rods.

If gross discrepancies show up on our measuring rods we conclude that intensities differ.[4]

Suppose one group of citizens in a town wants more schools even if this means higher property taxes for themselves, and another group wants low property taxes, even if this means crowded schools. Members in both groups, let us suppose, believe they have about a 50–50 chance of winning at the town meeting if they do nothing at all before the meeting. Suppose that the partisans of more schools sacrifice time, energy, leisure, and convenience to make their case known; speech and manner are marked by tension, frustration, irritation, anger, anxiety. The partisans of lower taxes, however, are unexcited and even apathetic and are heard to remark in private that a rise in the tax rate is not going to hurt them, but they feel they had better protest just to keep the PTA people from running away with the town. I think most of us will conclude that, although a number of alternative explanations present themselves (such as the possibility that the school advocates really like to organize and agitate), it is not unreasonable to say that the PTA group prefers schools over low taxes more than their opponents prefer low taxes over schools.

Several conclusions are, I believe, indicated by the discussion so far:

1. Most of us appear to believe that we can make comparisons of intensities.

2. We do so by postulating certain types of overt behavior as crude measures of intensities.

3. But we can do no more than postulate. We can never directly observe sensate intensities of want or preference; hence we can never know what the overt behavior we use as a measure really measures, unless it measures other kinds of overt behavior.

4. Even in the best of circumstances, where a variety of our postulated measuring rods seem to reveal crude differences in sensate intensity, alternative explanations are usually plausible.

5. However, "intensity" can be defined simply by reference to some observable response, such as a statement of one's feelings, willingness to give up leisure, etc.

4. For a more formal statement see Appendix C to this chapter. In some respects my argument parallels that of I. D. M. Little, *A Critique of Welfare Economics* (Oxford: Oxford University Press, 1950). However, compare pp. 55–59 with my argument above and in Appendix C.

6. If intensity is restricted to observable responses, then in principle A's intensity can be compared with B's.

7. Whether this is a satisfactory disposition of the intensity problem, however, depends upon the kind of decision we are required to make.

What, now, about our two problems? As to the first, the ethical problem, evidently the kind of intensity at stake is sensate. Hence, strictly speaking, we cannot construct any method for measuring or comparing different intensities in this sense. Only if we agree to regard some observable behavior as equivalent to sensate intensity can we begin to grapple with the problem at all. But many people will undoubtedly feel that in this case a solution to the problem with which we began has really eluded us and the use of overt behavior only begs the question.

Our second problem, the problem of stability, is of a different kind. For we are concerned with how people in the political system "feel" only so that we can predict how they are likely to act If we can predict how they are likely to act from observations of other overt behavior, then we do not need to worry ourselves with the question whether we really know how they feel. In principle, then, the problem seems capable of solution,[5] though it must be recorded that social science has not yet caught up with this problem. How stability varies in a democratic system with different distributions of preferences and intensities is a question that has scarcely been touched, except perhaps in a highly speculative fashion.

IV

Let us now assume that:

1. We can somehow determine overt intensities, that is, we derive a kind of "intensity scale" from overt behavior that will enable us to predict types of future political activity that influence the stability of the democratic system.

2. A case of "severe asymmetrical disagreement" exists; that is, a majority slightly prefers one alternative, and a minority strongly prefers a mutually exclusive alternative.

3. We wish to construct a set of rules or procedures that will facilitate a choice among the alternatives.

5. Cf. S. A. Stouffer *et al.*, *Measurement and Prediction*, Vol. IV of *Studies in Social Psychology in World War II* (Princeton: Princeton University Press, 1950), chaps. ii, iii, vi, vii, viii.

4. The rules must take not merely numbers of individuals into account—as in a pure majority rule—but also the intensity of their preferences.

5. The rules must operate so as to permit a minority veto over the majority only in cases where a relatively apathetic majority would, under pure majority rule, be able to override a relatively more intense minority. That is, the rule must be designed to distinguish the case of "severe asymmetrical disagreement" from the other distributions and permit a minority veto in that case only.

A word about the last requirement. If a decision carried by a relatively indifferent majority against the relatively strong preference of a minority is thought to be dangerous to stability (or ethically undesirable) then surely we must also regard as dangerous (or ethically undesirable) any decision in which (1) the minority gets its way by blocking the majority and (2) the number of individuals in the majority with a strong preference is equal to or greater than the number in the minority with an equally strong preference.

Without necessarily laying down a set of Utopian requirements, is it possible to design a set of rules to meet these specifications, at least in a crude way?[6] Since it is the Rule of populistic theory that creates the problem in the first place, it might be thought that an answer could be found in a kind of neo-Madisonian position. To the question, "How can we restrain a nearly indifferent majority from imposing its preference on a highly intense minority?" neo-Madisonian theory might be read as answering:

First, by a system of prescribed constitutional rules supplemented by organizational practices and procedures at key stages in the decision process—in political parties, elections, legislative activity, and judicial control, for example—so that an influential minority at any of these stages may veto the alternative preferred by a majority.

Second, by a social system of such diverse interests that instances of severe asymmetrical disagreement are unlikely to arise.

6. The economist, concerned as he is with "maximizing" behavior, would probably begin the other way round, i.e., he would set out to describe perfect attainment and then, perhaps, settle for some crude approximation. But as Herbert Simon has suggested, a more useful concept of rational choice is to be discovered in the concept of "satisfactory payoff," as distinct from a maximum or optimum payoff. Cf. his "A Behavioral Model of Rational Choice," *Quarterly Journal of Economics,* LIX (February, 1955), 99–118, esp. 108 ff.

Let us examine both of these briefly. As to the first, what guaranty does it provide that the fifth condition will be met—that the veto will be used only in cases of severe asymmetrical disagreement?

It would be challenging to design alternative sets of procedures in an effort to discover whether any among them would distinguish the case of severe asymmetrical disagreement from all others. However, let us content ourselves with the more modest question whether the set of constitutional and political procedures used in the making of decisions in the national government of the United States does in fact operate to distinguish this case. The only way we can answer that formidable question—if, indeed, we can answer it at all—is to take a brief look at some of the basic arrangements and the beneficiaries thereof; we shall return to this problem in Section V.

The second proposition has been defended in three ways. First, Madison's own defense seems to imply that, given sufficient diversity of interests and a large enough geographical area, no majorities can be organized and made effective in national decisions. But if this were true then no additional rules and procedures would be necessary; social checks and balances would be sufficient without superimposing additional constitutional checks and balances. A second line of defense is, however, that while a social system of diverse interests makes persistent majorities very difficult to organize, it does not render them impossible. Therefore a fuller guaranty is provided against majority tyranny if sufficient procedural checks are added so that any tentative majority will break itself against the successive constitutional and other political barriers. Here again we must ask whether these constitutional barriers distinguish the case of severe asymmetrical agreement from the others, or do they arbitrarily benefit some minorities at the expense of other minorities or possible majorities? We can only answer this by examining the particular arrangements and the particular beneficiaries.

The third defense, a popular one among American political scientists, draws upon the hypothesis of overlapping memberships. If most individuals in the society identify themselves with more than one group, then there is some positive probability that any majority contains individuals who identify themselves for certain purposes with the threatened minority. Members of the threatened minority who strongly prefer their alternative will make their feelings known to these members of the tentative majority who also, at some psychological level, identify themselves with the minority. Some of these sympathizers will shift their support away from the majority alternative and the majority will crumble.

Although, so far as I know, nothing except the most fragmentary evidence exists for this ingenious hypothesis, it is highly plausible; and I hope that before it becomes an unchallenged axiom of American political science it will at least be examined with some empirical rigor. For our purposes, it is important to note that if the hypothesis is true, then, in all the instances to which it applies, no further rules or procedures are necessary. If, however, there are instances of severe asymmetrical disagreement to which it does not apply, then it is appropriate to ask whether the particular set of rules and procedures making up American politics will provide a solution. We now turn to this question.

V

Among the overt constitutional arrangements to which Americans accede, three suggest themselves as possible solutions to our problem. The first is judicial review of legislation combined with a minority veto over constitutional amendments. The second is the structure of the Senate. The third consists of certain relations between the President, the two houses of Congress, and the electorate. We shall consider only the first two in this chapter.

It is appropriate to point out here that all three arrangements are usually defended by a style of argument so essentially Madisonian that I have, throughout these essays, named it as such. Nevertheless, at the Convention Madison himself was strongly opposed to the equal representation of states in the Senate, even if he finally acquiesced to it as the only possible compromise; and his suggestions for constitutional review provided for a council of revision that could have been overridden by a simple majority vote of Congress. Yet there is a certain justice in speaking of the whole system of constitutional restraints as Madisonian. For if Madison could grow indignant over the power of minorities when he thought of the great state of Virginia being set on a par with Delaware in the Senate, because his nice distinctions were at bottom arbitrary it was inevitable that his general argument should in time add stature to all the defenses against unlimited majority rule that were written into and about the Constitution.

Judicial review derives its strategic importance from the difficulties of altering the Constitution by formal amendment. As is well known, one-third plus one of the voting members of either house can prevent an amendment; if the amendment passes that barrier, one-fourth plus one of the states can veto it. Consequently if the Supreme Court vetoes legislation supported by even a substantial majority of the electorate, it by no means follows that the disappointed majority can then amend the Constitution. Conversely, if the Constitution permitted easy amendment by majorities, then most of the advantages of judicial review set forth by its advocates would also disappear. Hence we cannot consider judicial review independent of the amending power.

Although we can rarely be sure that a majority of the electorate actually favors a given controversial policy, in the case of child labor legislation the evidence that a majority favored national legislation is about as good as we are likely to find. In 1916 a Democratic Congress passed the first child labor law in the nation's history by a vote of 337–46 in the House and 52–12 in the Senate. Two years later, the Supreme Court held the law unconstitutional by a vote of 5–4. Within eight months a newly elected Republican Congress passed a new child labor law by a vote of 312–11 in the House and 50–12 in the Senate.[7] Three years later the Supreme Court held that law unconstitutional by a vote of 8–1. A constitutional amendment was thereupon introduced in the Congress; in 1924 it passed the House by a vote of 297–69 and the Senate by a vote of 61–23. After some initial rejections and some subsequent reversals, within twelve years the legislatures of twenty-four states with over 50 per cent of the population of the United States

7. In the Senate the vote was on the child labor amendment to the Revenue Bill for 1919; the vote on the entire Revenue Bill was 41–22. In the House the vote was on the entire Revenue Bill; no separate vote on the amendment was recorded.

had passed the amendment. By 1938, twenty-eight states with 55.6 per cent of the population had passed the amendment.[8] In that year, Congress passed the Fair Labor Standards Act, which included provisions outlawing child labor. In 1942 the Supreme Court upheld the measure. Thus by all the tests we can possibly employ, it seems fair to say that for over twenty years a legislative majority favored child labor legislation; and while the inference is more hazardous, it is likely that a majority of the electorate also favored child labor legislation. Yet because a minority of the national legislature, and probably a minority of the electorate, were supported by Supreme Court decisions, they were able to exercise an effective veto on child labor laws.

Does the Supreme Court's veto over Congressional legislation provide an answer to our problem of protecting the intense minority from the apathetic majority?[9] It should be said at once that the Court's defenders do not make this distinction. On the contrary, in the view of the Court and its partisans, it is precisely the intense law-making majority against which the rights of minorities must be defended. Joseph Choate enunciated a common conception of the Court's proper role when during his attack on the income tax in 1895 he said:

. . . If it be true, as my learned friend said in closing, that the passions of the people are aroused on this subject, if it be true that a mighty army of sixty million citizens is likely to be incensed by this decision, it is the more vital to the future welfare of this country that this Court again resolutely and courageously declare, as Marshall did, that it has the power to set aside an act of Congress violative of the Constitution, and that it will not hesitate in executing that power, no matter what the threatened consequences of popular or populistic wrath may be.[10]

Is it nevertheless reasonable to say that the process of judicial review of national legislation has in fact provided an effective protection for intense minorities against the invasions of apathetic majorities and

8. Cf. Appendix A to this chapter for a comment on the significance of the amending process as a guide to the existence of a majority.

9. In what follows I have deliberately excluded the question of judicial veto of state legislation. This involves a rather different set of issues, and examination of the record might well lead to a different set of conclusions.

10. Quoted in Carl Brent Swisher, *American Constitutional Development* (2d ed.; Boston: Houghton Mifflin Co., 1954), p. 448.

at the same time has not prevented relatively intense majorities from attaining their goals? If this were so, then the Court would constitute a nice solution to the problem of severe asymmetrical disagreement.

Now it is clear that we cannot answer this question unless we can first distinguish an apathetic majority from and intense one. But how can we do so? In the first place, how can we be sure what constitutes majority preference? Until quite recently we have had no opinion polls—at least, no scientific ones. In the absence of scientific pre-election opinion surveys, popular votes cast in national elections provide little guide, for issues entering into campaigns are always so complex that only by the wildest inference could we relate the percentage of votes cast for President directly to, say, a specific piece of legislation.[11] If even today—with the elaborate techniques of sounding public opinion now available to us—we cannot be at all sure of the relative importance of various issues, candidates, and voting habits in the immediately preceding election, how much more must this be so in the elections of a generation or a century ago?

I believe, therefore, that at present we can rarely speak with any reliability about majority preference in national elections of preceding decades. Usually all that we can properly say is that a given piece of legislation passed or failed each house by a given percentage of the votes and was signed or vetoed by the President. Hence in what follows we shall only speak of a law-making majority in the very restricted sense just indicated, i.e., a majority of the voting members of both houses plus presidential acquiescence.

If it is difficult to determine majority preferences on a specific piece of legislation, it is even more difficult to determine whether a hypothetical majority was relatively intense or apathetic. Perhaps the only available test is the extent to which efforts were made to repass the legislation, to amend the Constitution, to alter the Supreme Court's

11. This point is further developed in chapter 5, pp. 124 ff. It should be said that careful election studies employing census and other data, and using good if not elaborate statistical techniques, might do a great deal to give us a reasonably reliable reconstruction of some of the key determinants of past elections. Some studies of this kind are in progress at the Bureau of Applied Social Research, Columbia University. I doubt whether most of the standard historical explanations for electoral victory and defeat will stand up under this kind of inquiry.

jurisdiction, to pack the Court, and otherwise to bring about a new outcome. In this limited sense only, we may properly say that law-making majorities for the income tax or against child labor were probably not apathetic.

In the same restricted sense we can speak of a law-making minority, without always knowing whether it expresses only minority preferences among the electorate, and we can try to determine its intensity by its activities and persistence.

It is all too clear, I am afraid, that when we restrict ourselves to reliable inferences, we cannot talk with much confidence about our problem. This, in fact, is perhaps the most significant conclusion we can make. For if we are looking for a set of procedures to protect intense minorities against apathetic majorities; and if one possible set of arrangements is defended by an appeal to past experience; and if the past experience is shown to be irrelevant because we cannot interpret it with any reliability; then we must regard the attempts to defend these particular arrangements as mostly arbitrary prejudices.

Nonetheless, it may be useful to see what tentative conclusions we can derive from our historical experience with the Supreme Court. Over its whole history, the Supreme Court has held Congressional legislation unconstitutional in seventy-seven cases.[12] In almost one-third of these cases the aims of the original Congressional legislation were subsequently achieved by other means; in one-fifth of the cases the subsequent action took place in four years or less.[13] In at least four cases, more than twenty years were required. The most extreme instance of the judicial veto is child labor legislation, where twenty-six years intervened between the first law-making majority and the final

12. United States, Library of Congress, Legislative Reference Service, *Provisions of Federal Law Held Unconstitutional by the Supreme Court* (Washington, 1936), p. 95. Since this compilation, the only additional decision is *United States* v. *Lovett*, 328 U.S. 303 (1946).

13. My computations here are somewhat different from those on pages 135–36 of the Library of Congress document cited in note 12. However, many of the cases which the author of that document includes under other headings should be really considered as instances where the original object was achieved. Thus while it is technically correct to say that there was "no legislative action in response to decision" after *Dred Scott* v. *Sandford*, it would be false to say that the effects of that decision were not subsequently overcome.

consent of the Supreme Court. National legislation on workmen's compensation for longshoremen and harbor workers required twenty-five years and three different laws, one by a Democratic Congress in 1917, one by a Republican Congress in 1922, and the third by a Republican Congress in 1927. To attain our income tax took nineteen years, two different laws, and a constitutional amendment.[14]

In the remaining two-thirds of the cases where the ends were not subsequently achieved by other means, a considerable number involved temporary legislation and a large number involved essentially trivial or minor aspects of the legislation. There is, I believe, no case on

TABLE 1

TERMS OF OFFICE OF SUPREME COURT JUSTICES

Years	Percentage	Cum. Percentage
1–4.	9.2	9.2
5–8.	21.8	31.0
9–12.	14.9	45.9
13–16.	14.9	60.8
17–20.	8.1	68.9
21–24.	11.5	80.4
25–28.	9.2	89.6
29–32.	5.8	95.4
33–36.	4.6	100.0
	100.0	

record where a persistent law-making majority has not, sooner or later, achieved its purposes.

The great assets of the persistent law-making majority are senescence and death. The Supreme Court endures; judges are merely mortal. In the history of the Court, on the average one new justice has been appointed every twenty-three months. Thus a law-making majority has a reasonable chance of appointing two new members in one presidential term and four members in two presidential terms. Over 30 per cent of all justices have served eight years or less. The median is fifteen years (see Table 1). Since the President and the Senate

14. For a discussion of the Civil Rights cases, see Appendix B to this chapter.

scrutinize carefully the views of appointees to the Court and since the appointees are usually members of the dominant party or sympathetic to its views, it is not surprising that sooner or later "the Supreme Court follows the election returns."[15] What is surprising is that the interval is, in some cases, so long.

Turning back to the problem with which we began, what conclusions can we reasonably come to? I think the evidence indicates that:

1. In about two-thirds of the cases where the Supreme Court has held federal legislation unconstitutional, we can infer that the law-making majority was not intense. At any rate, it made no subsequent effort to achieve the purposes of the legislation in other ways.

2. Even in these cases, however, we have no way of knowing whether the minority protected by the Court was in some sense more intense in its preferences, unless we are prepared to say that, by definition, carrying the case to the courts is a sufficient indication of relative intensity.

3. In all the remaining cases, or about one-third of the total, the effects of the veto were overcome by other means—in one instance, by a civil war.

4. But in some of these cases, including the income tax, child labor, workmen's compensation, the regulation of the hours and wages of women, and others, the Supreme Court effectively delayed an apparently intense law-making majority for as much as a quarter of a century.

Thus we cannot conclude that the system of judicial review with restrictions on constitutional amendment constitutes a process that effectively prevents the preferences of relatively intense minorities from being overridden by relatively apathetic majorities without, at

15. Cf. Earl Latham, "The Supreme Court and the Supreme People," *Journal of Politics*, XVI (May, 1954), 207; Cortez A. M. Ewing, *The Judges of the Supreme Court, 1789–1937* (Minneapolis: University of Minnesota Press, 1938), chap. ii, examines the more controversial nominations. A thorough attack on judicial review as a means of protecting minority rights is Henry Steele Commager, *Majority Rule and Minority Rights* (New York: Oxford University Press, 1943). Fred Cahill, *Judicial Legislation* (New York: Ronald Press, 1952), examines the main intellectual efforts that have attempted to reconcile the patent fact that the Supreme Court is a legislative body with the theory that it is not; cf. especially chap. iii.

the same time, also restraining relatively intense majorities—that is, it fails to meet our fifth requirement. We cannot, then, look to the Supreme Court for a solution.

VI

Probably no one has argued with greater force against the desirability of equal representation of the states in the Senate than did James Madison at the Constitutional Convention; Madison said very nearly all that needs to be said about the fundamental contradiction between "the republican principle" and equal representation not of individuals but of geographical entities. In the end Madison accepted equal representation as a compromise necessary to secure the adherence of the small states to the new federal system. He viewed the compromise entirely as a matter not of principle but of desperate expedience. In the intervening years an expedient compromise has been converted into a principle, and Madison's own political theory has been used to justify it. Equal representation in the Senate, it is often said, is a device for protecting minorities against tyrannical majorities. In the context of these essays, can we interpret this to mean that equal representation in the Senate provides a solution for our problem of severe asymmetrical disagreement, where a relatively intense minority is faced with a relatively indifferent majority?[16]

As in the case of judicial review, the attempt to answer this question on the basis of the evidence runs into very formidable obstacles. It is clear at once that the criteria we used to distinguish intensity and relative indifference no longer apply, and I am not at all sure that any suitable criteria can be discovered. Even the attempt to distinguish situations in which the Senate protects a minority (presumably against the policies supported by the President or by a majority of votes in the House) is very difficult. Thus one conclusion we can certainly arrive at is that whatever may be the facts of the case, the attempt to defend the Senate as a mechanism for solving the intensity problem is bound

16. I am assuming that, as in the case of judicial review, the attempt to defend the arrangement on the grounds of natural rights runs into the difficulties indicated in chap 1.

to rest upon highly uncertain arguments incapable, even at best, of commanding more than the most tentative agreement.

Perhaps the only way to proceed is by examining, so far as may be possible, the kinds of minorities that are in some sense "overrepresented" in the Senate in order to discover, if we can, whether equal representation does operate to solve, or at any rate to mitigate, the problem of severe asymmetrical disagreement. Three observations should, however, be made at once. In the first place, the argument for equal representation of states in the Senate frequently seems to rest upon a false psychological equation, in which small states are equated with "small interests" and small interests with "small" or defenseless persons. Our humanitarian desires to protect relatively defenseless persons from aggression by more powerful individuals are thereby invoked on behalf of small states. But states consist of people; and it is the interests of people we are concerned with. What we want to know, therefore, is what sorts of people are benefited or handicapped by equal representation in the Senate.

I assume that we do not wish to indorse the principle that all small interest-groups must have a veto on policy. For then we could never specify any situations short of unanimity in which a law-making majority should be permitted to act. And thus we would make impossible not merely the operation of "the republican principle" but government itself. The first to exercise their vetoes might be the gangsters, the murderers, the thieves—in short, the criminal population. The rest of us would not be far behind: capitalists, laborers, farmers, even college professors, the exploiters and the exploited, the social and the anti-social, the sweatshop operator, the labor racketeer, the draft dodger, the income tax evader, and a thousand other groups, would exercise their veto on public policy. Certainly we should soon find ourselves with "no arts, no letters, no society, and which is worst of all, continual fear and danger of violent death, and the life of man solitary, poor, nasty, brutish, and short."

In the second place, we must also avoid the fallacy of assuming that if the Senate represents or overrepresents some minorities situated in

TABLE 2

	State Electorate* (000)	Percentage of Total Electorate	Cumulative Percentage	Index of Advantage†
1. Nevada............	81	.14	.14	14.8
2. Wyoming.........	127	.22	.36	9.4
3. Vermont..........	153	.27	.63	7.8
4. Delaware.........	170	.30	.93	7.0
5. North Dakota.....	231	.40	1.33	5.2
6. New Mexico.......	233	.41	1.74	5.1
7. Maine............	234	.41	2.15	5.1
8. Mississippi........	240	.42	2.57	5.0
9. Arizona..........	248	.43	3.00	4.8
10. Montana..........	256	.45	3.45	4.7
11. New Hampshire...	258	.45	3.90	4.6
12. Idaho............	264	.46	4.36	4.5
13. South Carolina....	284	.49	4.85	4.2
14. South Dakota.....	287	.50	5.35	4.2
15. Utah.............	326	.57	5.92	3.7
16. Alabama..........	342	.59	6.51	3.5
17. Arkansas.........	361	.63	7.14	3.3
18. Rhode Island......	407	.71	7.85	2.9
19. Louisiana.........	416	.72	8.57	2.9
20. Virginia..........	447	.78	9.35	2.7
21. Georgia..........	547	.95	10.30	2.2
22. Nebraska.........	566	.98	11.28	2.1
23. Colorado.........	606	1.06	12.34	2.0
24. Oregon...........	666	1.16	13.50	1.8
25. Tennessee........	700	1.22	14.72	1.7
26. Florida..........	739	1.28	16.00	1.6
27. Kansas...........	824	1.43	17.43	1.46
28. Maryland.........	841	1.46	18.89	1.43
29. West Virginia.....	874	1.52	20.41	1.37
30. Oklahoma........	933	1.63	22.04	1.28
31. Kentucky.........	951	1.66	23.70	1.26
32. Washington.......	1016	1.77	25.47	1.18
33. Connecticut.......	1093	1.90	27.37	1.1
34. North Carolina....	1122	1.95	29.32	1.08
35. Iowa.............	1143	1.99	31.31	1.05
36. Minnesota........	1388	2.41	33.72	0.86
37. Wisconsin........	1568	2.73	36.45	0.76
38. Texas............	1719	2.99	39.44	0.70
39. Missouri.........	1861	3.24	42.68	0.64
40. Indiana..........	1935	3.37	46.15	0.62
41. Massachusetts.....	2289	3.98	50.03	0.52

* Votes cast for U.S. Representatives, 1952. Source: *Statistics of the Presidential and Congressional Election of November 4, 1952* (Washington, D.C.: U.S. Government Printing Office, 1953).

† Index of advantage $= \dfrac{\text{actual representation}}{\text{proportionate representation}}$

$= \dfrac{1}{48} \Big/ \dfrac{\text{state electorate}}{\text{total electorate}}$

$= \dfrac{\text{mean state electorate}}{\text{state electorate}} = \dfrac{1,199,000}{\text{state electorate}}$

If actual representation = proportionate representation, then the index of advantage = 1.

TABLE 2—*Continued*

	State Electorate* (000)	Percentage of Total Electorate	Cumulative Percentage	Index of Advantage†
42. New Jersey........	2315	4.03	54.06	0.52
43. Michigan.........	2772	4.82	58.88	0.43
44. Ohio.............	3382	5.88	64.76	0.36
45. Illinois..........	4352	7.57	72.33	0.28
46. Pennsylvania.....	4507	7.84	80.17	0.27
47. California........	4563	7.93	88.10	0.26
48. New York........	6910	12.01	100.11‡	0.17
Total..............	57,559			
Mean.............	1,199			

‡ The total is more than 100 per cent because of rounding.

certain geographical areas in the United States, it necessarily represents all minorities situated in those areas. This is clearly false. There are minorities within minorities. The dominant regional group may be represented in the Senate while the subordinate regional minority is excluded. Hence a Senate veto may merely preserve or extend the control of the dominant regional group over the subordinate minority. The Negroes in the South, the itinerant farm laborers of the West, the wetbacks of the Southwest; these are clearly not the minorities who benefit from equal representation in the Senate. It is worth remembering that even in a situation of full political equality, a regional minority protected by equal representation of geographical units in a legislative body would be a majority in its own area; and the defeated minority in that region would be unprotected by equal representation. Indeed, if the minority in the region consisted of individuals with preferences like those of the majority in the whole electorate, equal representation of geographical areas would, paradoxically, divest this regional minority of protection in all cases where positive government action was required to prevent the regional majority from tyrannizing over it.

In the third place, equal representation of geographical units overrepresents some minorities concentrated in sparse areas but underrepresents those concentrated in heavily populated areas. Moreover, to the extent that a minority is not geographically concentrated, it receives no protection per se from equal state representation. In a society in which all minorities were distributed in equal proportions among the voters of every state, no minority would receive any protection per se from equal state representation. Why, then, this special tenderness toward minorities concentrated geographically in sparse areas? Although a perfectly good historical answer can be found, it is not an answer that can be easily rationalized as a solution to our problem of severe asymmetrical disagreement.

If we are concerned simply with the extent to which the electorate rather than the whole population is represented then it is perhaps best to rank states by the number of voters.[17] In Table 2 all the states are ranked according to the number of votes cast for candidates for the United States House of Representatives in the 1952 election. It will be seen that the eight largest states with 54 per cent of the voters have the same number of votes in the Senate as the eight smallest states with less than 3 per cent of the voters. A majority of votes in the Senate can be cast by Senators representing less than 15 per cent of the voters. Thus a policy preferred by the representatives of 85 per cent of the voters could be vetoed by the representatives of 15 per cent of the voters. Nevada has nearly fifteen times as much representation as it would have if representation were apportioned strictly according to the number of voters. New York has only one-sixth as much representation as it would have if voters were equally represented. Thus an average vote cast in Nevada has eighty-five times as much weight as an average vote cast in New York, other things being equal. Thirty-five states are overrepresented,[18] and thirteen are underrepresented. Twenty-three states have more than twice their proportionate representation, and each of the eight largest states has half or less than half of its proportionate representation.

So much for the extent of the discrepancy. What groups might be benefited or disadvantaged by equal representation? In Table 3 are

17. The rankings would not be significantly different.

18. Meaning more representation than the state would have if voters were represented equally.

three groups who, it is fair to say, have not been among the dominant forces in their states and have not been protected—they have even been disadvantaged—by equal state representation. However, in Table 3.1 are a number of groups whose interests may have been furthered by overrepresentation. In Table 3.2 is another set of groups

TABLE 3

(1) No. of States	(2) Percentage of States	(3) Percentage of Total Voters*	(4) Relative Advan- tage†	(5) Group	(6) Percentage of Group in these States‡
9+D.C...	18.8	7.8	2.4	Negroes	50.0
11.........	22.8	13.2	1.7	Sharecroppers	68.0
8.........	16.7	12.5	1.3	Migrant workers§	33.0

* Votes cast for U.S. House of Representatives, November, 1952.
† $\frac{\text{Col. (2)}}{\text{Col. (3)}}$.
‡ Source: 1950 census: Vital statistics and census of agriculture.
§ Those working over 150 days off the farm.

TABLE 3.1

No. of States	Percentage of States	Percentage of Total Voters	Relative Advantage	Group	Percentage of Group in These States
8.........	16.7	9.2	1.8	Farmers	35.4
7.........	14.6	6.2	2.4	Wool shorn (lbs.)	57.6
6.........	12.5	5.0	2.5	Cotton farms	67.0
4.........	8.3	1.9	4.4	Silver mined	84.4

Sources: 1950 census; census of agriculture; Bureau of Mines, *Minerals Yearbook*.

TABLE 3.2

No. of States	Percentage of States	Percentage of Total Voters	Relative Advantage	Group	Percentage of Group in These States
12.........	25.0	51.0	0.49	Wage earners	53.7
2.........	4.2	9.4	0.45	Coal miners	58.8

Sources: 1950 census: Characteristics of the population.

whose interests may have been disadvantaged by underrepresentation.

Now the interesting thing about these tables is that the groups benefited and handicapped by equal representation seem entirely arbitrary. It would be difficult to argue that either natural rights or relative intensities requires the underrepresentation of Negroes, share-croppers, migrant workers, wage earners, and coal miners and the overrepresentation of farmers and wool, cotton, and silver producers.

In sum:

1. The only minorities protected by equal state representation as such are geographical minorities concentrated in sparse areas.

2. But some of the minorities in these areas are left unprotected; indeed, representatives of the dominant group may actually use their overrepresentation in the Senate to bar action intended to guard the unprotected.

3. Minorities in heavily populated areas are underrepresented in a system of equal state representation.

4. It is impossible to determine the relative intensities of these various groups, but the conclusion seems inevitable that the benefits and disadvantages are allocated in an entirely arbitrary fashion and cannot be shown to follow from any general principle.

I do not mean to suggest that the Connecticut Compromise should be undone; but I do mean to say that it is rather muddleheaded to romanticize a necessary bargain into a grand principle of democratic politics.

VII

What conclusions can we come to, then, about the intensity problem?

First, however strongly we may believe sensate intensity to be a fact, we cannot directly observe and measure interpersonal differences in sensations. Hence we cannot hope to establish any political rules to deal with problems of sensate intensity, ethically desirable as such rules possibly might be.

Second, in so far as we may be content to define intensity in terms of activities we can observe, in principle it should be possible to compare the relative intensities of preference among different individuals.

Third, given various possible distributions of different intensities among a majority and a minority, several do not seem to raise significant problems for democratic theory. For at least one distribution no democratic solution seems possible. A final case does, however, raise some interesting questions, namely, any situation where a relatively intense minority prefers an alternative opposed by a relatively apathetic majority.

Fourth, although it has sometimes been suggested that the American constitutional system is peculiarly designed to deal with this third case, neither judicial review nor the equal representation of the states in the Senate provides a solution.

Finally, the analysis strongly suggests, although it does not prove, that no solution to the intensity problem through constitutional or procedural rules is attainable.

APPENDIX TO CHAPTER 4

A. Majorities and the amending process

It is worth noting that amendment by some proportion of the geographical units of a country, e.g., the states, in itself neither prohibits a bare majority of the electorate from amending the constitution nor guarantees that a bare majority will be sufficient to do so. To show this, let us assume that (*a*) the legislatures of each state are perfectly attuned to the preferences of a majority of the electorate in that state, (*b*) the population is equally distributed among the states, (*c*) the legislatures of three-fourths of the states must approve the amendment if it is to be adopted, and (*d*) three-fourths of the state legislatures approve the amendment and one-fourth disapprove. Then a formula can easily be constructed showing all the situations in which a majority of the national electorate does or does not favor the amendment. Let x be the percentage of the electorate favoring the amendment in each of the three-fourths of the states whose legislatures approve the amendment, and y the percentage of the electorate favoring the amendment in the remaining one-fourth of the states whose legislatures oppose the amendment. Under assumption (*a*) above, x must always be greater than, and y less than, 50. Then for a majority of the entire electorate to favor the amendment requires:

$$y > 200 - 3x.$$

Hence if y is equal to or less than this amount, the amendment will be passed even though it is favored only by a minority of the national electorate.

Table 4 suggests some of the possible values:

TABLE 4

% Favorable in States Approving (y)	% Required in States Opposing (x)
50.01	49.97
50.1	49.7
51.0	47.0
52.0	44.0
53.0	41.0
66.0	2.0
66.66	0

Thus if a bare majority, say 51 per cent of the electorates of 36 states favor an amendment, under our assumptions, it will be adopted. Yet such an adoption is consistent both with the possibility that a bare majority of the entire national electorate supports the amendment and with the possibility that a majority of the entire national electorate opposes it. That is, if more than 47 per cent of the electorates of the remaining 12 states support the amendment, then a majority of the national electorate supports it. But if less than 47 per cent of the electorates in the remaining 12 states support the amendment, then it will be adopted even though only a minority of the national electorate supports it. (The percentages may be regarded either as percentages of the electorate in each of the states, or as arithmetic means, or as percentages of the total electorate in the states for and in the states against, respectively.)

The same argument may be used to show that even if the requirement were dropped to a bare majority of the states $(n/2 + 1)$ then the situation would be equally indeterminate, i.e., an amendment might be passed with majority support, or with less than majority support, or fail even though it has majority support.

If we eliminate our highly artificial assumption as to equal population or equal electorates in each of the states then the situation is even more erratic. For example, given the voting turnout of 1952 bare majorities in 36 states with 31.3 per cent of the electorate could, in principle, amend the Constitution; thus a Constitutional amendment would need to have the support of only 16 per cent of the total electorate. On the other hand, the 63 per cent of the electorate concentrated in 11 states could neither amend the Constitution nor impose a veto on a proposed amendment.

The point of all this is not to show that these events actually occur or are likely to occur. It is merely to show that a method of amendment based upon approval by geographical units does not per se lead to any determinate answer as to whether a majority can or cannot amend the Constitution.

B. *The Supreme Court and Negro rights*

It might be argued that the six cases dealing with post–Civil War legislation extending and protecting the rights of Negroes should be cited as the outstanding example of frustration of a persistent law-making majority by the Supreme Court. But it is impossible to show that there was a Congressional majority to frustrate. The legislation was all passed during Grant's two terms, when the southern Democrats were still excluded from Congress and the radical Republicans were a powerful force. The first of the Supreme Court decisions occurred in 1876, and all of the others came later: two in 1883, and one each in 1887, 1903, and 1906. That the election of 1876 was a turning point in the "road to reunion" has long been recognized by historians; from that year on, the power of the white South in Congress was virtually restored. The bargaining that led up to the settlement, and the nature of the settlement itself, have recently been explored in detail by C. Vann Woodward in *Reunion and Reaction: The Compromise of 1877 and the End of Reconstruction* (Boston: Little, Brown & Co., 1951). The year 1876, then, marks the approximate point at which the dominant forces in the Republican party came to terms with the dominant forces in the South and agreed to tolerate, if not actually to support, a restoration of white supremacy. The last piece of legislation to protect the rights of southern Negroes passed a lame duck Congress in February, 1875, and was signed by the President on March 1. Three days later the terms of office of the Republican House expired; it was not until fifteen years later that the Republicans again were in effective control of the House. The Republican leadership merely acquiesced in white supremacy; the leaders of the Democratic party demanded it. During the period from 1875 to 1897 in all but four years the Democrats controlled at least one branch of the legislature. In four of the five presidential elections from 1876 to 1892, the Democratic candidate polled more popular votes than the Republican, although only twice was a Democrat elected. The decision of 1877 thus became a stable part of the bundle of fundamental compromises on which American politics has always depended. It was not until after World War II that the compromise was broken (if it ever was broken). Then, as is well known, southern Democrats used the filibuster in the Senate to veto the attempts of what might have amounted to a law-making majority to pass the legislation intended to protect the rights of Negro citizens and others. In the face of this veto by filibuster, it was the Supreme Court itself which, in its historic decision in 1954, legislated Negro rights back into the Constitution. Thus, paradoxically, the Supreme Court seems not to have been opposed to a law-making majority either when it took the rights of Negroes away or when it gave them back.

C. A note on the comparison of intensities of preference

Let us assume that a single continuum of sensate intensity exists, such that intensities can be ordered from lesser to greater:

Therefore if the intensity of preference of individual A is at x, his preference is less intense than that of individual B at y.

But since we cannot observe intensity, how can we know that individual A is at x and individual B is at y? Let us construct a scale, consisting, for example, of responses to the question: "Do you feel very strongly about this objective? Moderately? Indifferently?"

indifferent	moderate	strong
x'	y'	z'

→ scale

If this scale can be connected with another set of events in such a way that the relative order of a point (or a range) on the scale unambiguously indicates the relative order of a point (or a range) on the set of events, then the scale "measures" the set of events:

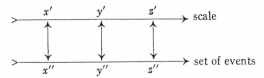

Let us suppose that we find empirically that our scale permits us to predict some other set of ordered events, e.g., the relative amount of leisure forgone by an individual to achieve the objective. That is, if individual A is at x' on the scale, he will be at x'' on the continuum of "leisure forgone"; and if B is at y' he will also be at y'':

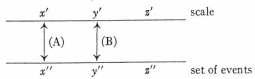

Several steps are now possible:

1. Although we cannot observe sensate intensities, we may agree to proceed as if sensate intensities are measured by this scale (or others):

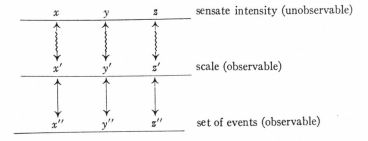

But note that although the scale and the set of events are both observable and related by observations, we have no observations to relate our scale, or the set of observable events, with sensate intensity. We merely "agree" that (*a*) sensate intensity exists and (*b*) our scale measures it. Narrowly interpreted, all that we have done, in effect, is to treat sensate intensity as a construct consisting of the outcome of a set of measurements of some observable items.

2. In view of this we may agree to abandon the construct "sensate intensity," i.e., for our purposes, we drop assumptions (*a*) and (*b*). We then treat our scale merely as a predictor for the observable set of events: if individual A is at x' then he will also be at x'' (or there is some known probability, P, that he will be at x''). We may, if we wish, label our scale an "intensity" scale, provided we read nothing into the label beyond the set of measurements.

If our concern is ethical and we are worried about sensate intensities, then 2 is unsatisfactory; but all solutions will, I think, be equally so. If our concern is empirical, e.g., if we are concerned with predicting the stability of a social organization, then 2 might be satisfactory, provided we can find a scale for the set of events we wish to predict.

CHAPTER 5

American Hybrid

Like a nagging tooth, Madison's problem of majority tyranny has persistently troubled us throughout these essays. As we discovered at the outset, it is no simple matter even to define the terms satisfactorily. If momentarily it appeared that an examination of "intensity" might give us an answer, in the end our exploration of intensity turned up no clear solution.

Nevertheless, from what has gone before, seven important propositions bearing on this issue may, I think, be developed. If these propositions are somewhat speculative, they are not merely consistent with all that has been argued so far but to a substantial degree are implicit in the argument.

I

The first of these propositions is that on matters of specific policy the majority rarely rules.

In analyzing polyarchal democracy we found it necessary to lay down seven separate conditions necessary to maximum attainment of the Rule during the election period, that is, we described seven continua against which the relative attainment of the Rule during the election period might be measured. This emphasis on the conditions of the election period is significant, for I think none of the developments in the past century and a half in understanding the operation of democratic societies, and certainly none of the recent developments in empirical political science should be interpreted as decreasing the critical role of elections in maximizing political equality and popular sovereignty. Although it is fashionable in some quarters to suggest that everything believed about democratic politics prior to World War I, and perhaps World War II, was nonsense, I am inclined to think that the radical democrats who, unlike Madison, insist upon the decisive importance of the election process in the whole grand strategy of democracy are essentially correct. To be sure, if the social prerequisites of polyarchy do not exist, then the election process cannot mitigate, avoid, or displace hierarchical government. But if the social prerequisites of polyarchy do exist, then the election is the critical technique for insuring that governmental leaders will be relatively responsive to non-leaders; other techniques depend for their efficacy primarily upon the existence of elections and the social prerequisites.

Having said so much, it is important to notice how little a national election tells us about the preferences of majorities. Strictly speaking, all an election reveals is the first preferences of some citizens among the candidates standing for office. Let us see what it does not do.

Let us put to one side the fact that because of election machinery the outcome may actually run counter to the expressed preferences of a plurality of voters; for example, in three national elections in the United States, the candidate preferred by the most voters was not made President. Let us also put to one side the fact that when more than two candidates run for office, the winning candidate may have a plurality but not a majority of votes; and it is usually impossible to say what the outcome would have been if there had been a run-off election between the two candidates with the highest number of votes. Thus in nine American presidential elections the winning candidate has had a plurality but not a majority of popular votes. Hence in twelve cases, or more than one-third of the presidential elections since Jackson,[1] the winning candidate has not been the first choice of a majority of voters.

Far more significant is the fact that even when a candidate is evi-

1. Before Jackson, presidential electors were usually chosen by state legislatures. Consequently it is difficult to estimate the number of voters who supported a given candidate; compilations of popular votes in presidential elections usually begin with the election of 1828.

dently a first choice of a majority of voters, we cannot be sure in a national election that he is also a first choice of a majority of adults or eligible voters.[2] Although the American case is extreme, in every nation state where compulsory voting does not exist the basic proposition holds. In any given election we are almost never in a position to know for sure what the outcome would have been if some or all of the non-voters had actually voted. We have slight reason to suppose that the outcome would have been the same. In a close election a small last minute rise in the proportion of voters drawn from those favorable to one of the sides can change the outcome; something like this seems to have happened in the last two weeks of the 1948 campaign.[3] Moreover, one of the sides is often handicapped by non-voting more than the other; for example, when non-voting is inversely related to income, education, and other related factors, in a close division of opinion the candidate of the poor and uneducated is more likely to lose, even when he is the first preference of all the adults or eligible voters, than is the candidate of the educated and the well-to-do. In the 1952 presidential election, it appears that about 20 per cent of those who favored Eisenhower did not vote, whereas about 29 per cent of those who favored Stevenson did not vote.[4] In a close division of opinion, the difference in the proportions of non-voters would have been crucial.[5]

2. However, modern sample surveys of public opinion are now helpful in this respect.

3. See *The Pre-Election Polls of 1948* (New York: Social Science Research Council, 1949); Angus Campbell and R. L. Kahn, *The People Elect a President* (Ann Arbor: Institute for Social Research, 1952); Angus Campbell, Gerald Gurin, and Warren E. Miller, *The Voter Decides* (Evanston: Row, Peterson & Co., 1954).

4. Campbell *et al.*, *op cit.*, p. 31, Table 3.2.

5. It can easily be shown that in order for the winning candidate to be the first choice of a majority of all eligible voters, he must also be the first choice of a percentage of the non-voters greater than: $(X-2W)/2Z$, where X is the number of eligible voters, W is the number of votes obtained by the winning candidate, and Z is the number of non-voters. For example, in 1948, Mr. Truman was the first choice of a majority of all eligible voters only if he was also the first choice of more than 50.7 per cent of the non-voters; in 1952, on the other hand, Mr. Eisenhower would only have needed the support of more than 41.2 per cent of the non-voters. The estimates are based on data in tables in: *The Political Almanac of 1952* (New York: Forbes & Sons, 1952), p. 22; *Statistics of the Presidential and Congressional Elections of Nov. 4, 1952* (Washington: Government Printing Office,

Now if all the non-voters were indifferent as to the outcome, then, according to our argument in chapter 2, their preferences, or lack of them, could be ignored in determining what a majority of adults prefer. But unfortunately it is not true that all non-voters are indifferent; for example, in one national sample studied in 1952, out of 450 persons who said they cared very much which party won the presidential election, 76 (or 17 per cent) evidently did not vote. Of the Stevenson supporters who "cared very much" about the outcome, a much higher percentage (28 per cent) failed to vote than among highly concerned Eisenhower supporters (10 per cent).[6]

Finally, in appraising the significance of elections as an indication of first choices, it must be remembered that a great many voters do not really perceive a choice between candidate A and candidate B; for many people the only perceived alternatives are to vote for one of the candidates or not to vote at all.[7]

Even if we could rule out all these difficulties, it would still be true that we can rarely interpret a majority of first choices among candidates in a national election as being equivalent to a majority of first choices for a specific policy. Some people evidently vote for a candidate although they are quite indifferent about the issues. Others support a candidate who is opposed to them on some issues; in the 1952 sample already referred to, 29 per cent of those who took a Democratic position on the Taft-Hartley Act nonetheless supported Eisenhower. Furthermore, the supporters of a candidate often differ widely in their preferences on issues. In one sample of those who supported Eisenhower in 1952, about 64 per cent thought the United States had gone too far in concerning itself with problems in other parts of the world,

1953), p. 52; and V. O. Key, *A Primer of Statistics for Political Scientists* (New York: Thomas Y. Crowell & Co., 1953), p. 197.

6. My estimates are based on the data in Table 3.8, Campbell *et al.*, *op. cit.*, p. 37.

7. In the 1948 election, in one sample of voters, 73 per cent said they had never thought of voting for the other candidate at any time during the campaign; in the 1952 election, in another sample of voters, the figure was 78 per cent, *ibid.*, p. 23, Table 2.7. This suggests the upper limit; the data do not indicate how many of these saw non-voting as an alternative to voting for their candidate.

about 27 per cent thought it had not, and about 9 per cent were neutral.[8] Thus it becomes possible for a resounding majority of the voters to elect a candidate all of whose policies are the first choices of only a minority.

Imagine, for example, that voters must choose between two candidates who disagree on three policies as set forth in Table 5. Now let us suppose that each of these minorities is a distinct group, so that together the three minorities make up 75 per cent of the voters. Let us suppose that the first minority regards foreign policy as the crucial issue and ranks its choices: u, x, z, w, y, v. That is, these voters prefer candidate A because he offers them a foreign policy of which they approve, even though they dislike his farm and fiscal policies. Now suppose that the second minority of voters regards farm policy as

TABLE 5

	Candidate A Prefers Alternative	Supported by	Candidate B Prefers Alternative	Supported by
Foreign policy...	u	25 per cent of voters	v	75 per cent of voters
Farm policy.....	w	25 per cent of voters	x	75 per cent of voters
Fiscal policy....	y	25 per cent of voters	z	75 per cent of voters

crucial and ranks its choices: w, z, v, u, y, x. That is, these voters prefer candidate A because he offers them a farm policy they like, even though they disapprove of his stand on foreign and fiscal policy. Applying the same kind of reasoning to the third minority, it can be readily seen that candidate A might win 75 per cent of the votes, even though each of his policies is opposed by 75 per cent of the voters. This is an instance, not of majority rule or even of minority rule, but of *minorities* rule.

In addition, in so far as voters prefer a candidate because of his policies, frequently the support represents approval or disapproval of a policy already enacted, even if little or nothing can be done to change the consequences of the policy. No doubt many people voted against

8. My estimates are based upon Table 8.1, *ibid.*

Stevenson in 1952 because Truman had not stopped the Chinese Communists in 1947.[9] The vote was more of a punishment for past action than a choice of future policy. Political leaders recognize this aspect of elections and frequently seek to avoid a decision until an election is over so that they may then act relatively free from campaign commitments. Thus paradoxically an election may actually prevent rather than facilitate policy choices by the electorate.

Now the unwary student of contemporary democracies may hastily conclude that the deficiencies in elections I have alluded to are characteristic only of the United States, but except for peculiarities that I agreed to put to one side as remediable in principle, what I have said applies with equal force, I believe, to the politics of any large nation state. Although political scientists sometimes appear to believe that many of the virtues and few of the vices of American politics are to be found in the English parliamentary system, operating with two highly unified and disciplined parties, I am inclined to think that elections under that system are, if anything, even less controlling than our own.[10] The only important point to stress here is that in no large nation state

9. 71 per cent of those who thought it "was our government's fault that China went Communistic" supported Eisenhower, *ibid.*

10. Great Britain furnishes an interesting confirmation of the fact that electoral majorities rarely determine specific policy. The British political system has few of the constitutional and political barriers to majority rule characteristic of the American system. Nevertheless, it is comparatively rare for the party in power to have been the first preference of a majority of the voters—much less of the whole electorate—at the preceding election. Since 1923 there have been nine elections. Only two of these indicated a majority of first preferences for the ensuing government. Even the two exceptions are politically aberrant. In the election of 1931, candidates endorsing Ramsay MacDonald's national coalition won a majority of the votes, the Labor party having been badly hit by MacDonald's withdrawal. In 1935, the Conservative party candidates won only 47.7 per cent of the votes, but candidates endorsing the National government won 54.7 per cent of the votes. Not since 1945 has any government been the first preference of a majority of the voters. Indeed, in 1945, 10.4 million people eligible to vote either did not vote or voted for candidates other than Labor or Conservative compared with 9.6 million for the Conservatives and 12 million for Labor candidates. In 1950, this group numbered 8.2 million, compared with 12.1 million Conservative voters and 13.2 million Labor voters. Cf. *The Constitutional Year Book, 1938* (London: Harrison, 1938), Vol. LII; D. E. Butler, *The Electoral System in Britain, 1918–1951* (Oxford: Clarendon Press, 1953), p. 173; John Bonham, *The Middle Class Vote* (London: Faber & Faber, 1955), p. 120.

can elections tell us much about the preferences of majorities and minorities, beyond the bare fact that among those who went to the polls a majority, plurality, or minority indicated their first choices for some particular candidate or group of candidates. What the first choices of this electoral majority are, beyond that for the particular candidates, it is almost impossible to say with much confidence.

What is true of elections must be even more true of the interelection period. Our polyarchal model tried to account for the interelection period by means of its eighth condition:

8.1. Either all interelections decisions are subordinate or executory to those arrived at during the election stage

8.2. Or new decisions during the interelection period are governed by the preceding seven conditions, operating, however, under rather different institutional circumstances

8.3. Or both.

The reader may have felt at the time that this was a sorry way to by-pass a formidable problem. I think so myself, but one cannot say everything at once.

We have just shown that condition 8.1 is, in practice, quite inadequately attained. The link between elections and policy choices is not feeble; but if an election rarely reveals the preferences of a majority on policy matters, there is no majority preference to which interelection decisions may be subordinate or executory. The other possible condition (8.2) meets with equally great difficulties, for most interelection policy seems to be determined by the efforts of relatively small but relatively active minorities. I believe there is no case in the whole history of American politics where interelection activity was at anything like the level of activity in an ordinary election. If you examine carefully any policy decision, even a very important one, you will always discover, I believe, that only a quite tiny proportion of the electorate is actively bringing its influence to bear upon politicians. In an area as critical as foreign policy, the evidence is conclusive that year in and year out the overwhelming proportion of American citizens makes its preferences effective, if at all, by no means other than going to the polls and casting a ballot. In a recent survey of American attitudes on world organization, the percentages of various opinion groups who reported that they had done nothing to spread their point of view, such as belonging to organizations, engaging in political activity, or even discussing their position with their friends, were as follows:[11]

Among "isolationists": 87 per cent
Among those favoring the United Nations as it is: 84 per cent
Among those favoing a stronger United Nations: 80 per cent
Among those supporting some kind of union among the democracies: 84 per cent

I am not suggesting that elections and interelection activity are of trivial importance in determining policy.[12] On the contrary, they are crucial processes for insuring that political leaders will be somewhat responsive to the preferences of some ordinary citizens. But neither elections nor interelection activity provide much insurance that decisions will accord with the preferences of a majority of adults or voters. Hence we cannot correctly describe the actual operations of democratic societies in terms of the contrasts between majorities and minorities. We can only distinguish groups of various types and sizes, all seeking in various ways to advance their goals, usually at the expense, at least in part, of others.[13]

II

I have shown both that elections are a crucial device for controlling leaders and that they are quite ineffective as indicators of majority preference. These statements are really not in contradiction. A good deal of traditional democratic theory leads us to expect more from national elections than they can possibly provide. We expect elections to reveal the "will" or the preferences of a majority on a set of issues. This is one thing elections rarely do, except in an almost trivial fashion. Despite this limitation the election process is one of two fundamental

11. Elmo Roper, "American Attitudes on World Organization," *Public Opinion Quarterly*, XVII (winter, 1953–54), pp. 405–20.

12. In this respect the otherwise excellent analysis of democracy in Joseph A. Schumpeter, *Capitalism, Socialism and Democracy* (2d ed.; New York: Harper & Bros., 1947), seems to me somewhat defective.

13. Arthur F. Bentley, *The Process of Government* (Chicago: University of Chicago Press, 1908); David Truman, *The Governmental Process* (New York: A. A. Knopf, Inc., 1951); Earl Latham, *The Groups Basis of Politics: A Study in Basing Point Legislation* (Ithaca: Cornell University Press, 1952).

methods of social control which, operating together, make governmental leaders so responsive to non-leaders that the distinction between democracy and dictatorship still makes sense. The other method
of social control is continuous political competition among individuals,
parties, or both. Elections and political competition do not make for
government by majorities in any very significant way, but they vastly
increase the size, number, and variety of minorities whose preferences
must be taken into account by leaders in making policy choices. I am
inclined to think that it is in this characteristic of elections—not
minority rule but minorities rule—that we must look for some of the
essential differences between dictatorships and democracies.

III

But there is another characteristic of elections that is important
for our inquiry. If the majority rarely rules on matters of specific
policy, nevertheless the specific policies selected by a process of
"minorities rule" probably lie most of the time within the bounds of
consensus set by the important values of the politically active members of the society, of whom the voters are a key group. This, then, is
our third proposition; and in this sense the majority (at least of the
politically active) nearly always "rules" in a polyarchal system. For
politicians subject to elections must operate within the limits set both
by their own values, as indoctrinated members of the society, and by
their expectations about what policies they can adopt and still be re-
elected.

In a sense, what we ordinarily describe as democratic "politics" is
merely the chaff. It is the surface manifestation, representing super-
ficial conflicts. Prior to politics, beneath it, enveloping it, restricting it,
conditioning it, is the underlying consensus on policy that usually
exists in the society among a predominant portion of the politically
active members. Without such a consensus no democratic system
would long survive the endless irritations and frustrations of elections
and party competition. With such a consensus the disputes over policy
alternatives are nearly always disputes over a set of alternatives that

have already been winnowed down to those within the broad area of basic agreement.

Lest anyone conclude that these basic agreements are trivial: a century ago in the United States it was a subject of political debate whether the enslavement of human beings was or was not desirable. Today this question is not subject to political debate.

IV

If majorities in a democracy nearly always govern in the broad meaning of the term, they rarely rule in Madison's terms: for as we have seen, specific policies tend to be products of "minorities rule." In the sense in which Madison was concerned with the problem then, majority rule is mostly a myth. This leads to our fourth proposition: If majority rule is mostly a myth, then majority tyranny is mostly a myth too. For if the majority cannot rule, surely it cannot be tyrannical.

The real world issue has not turned out to be whether a majority, much less "the" majority, will act in a tyrannical way through democratic procedures to impose its will on a (or the) minority. Instead, the more relevant question is the extent to which various minorities in a society will frustrate the ambitions of one another with the passive acquiescence or indifference of a majority of adults or voters.

That some minorities will frustrate and in that sense tyrannize over others is inherent in a society where people disagree, that is, in human society. But if frustration is inherent in human society, dictatorship is not. However, if there is anything to be said for the processes that actually distinguish democracy (or polyarchy) from dictatorship, it is not discoverable in the clear-cut distinction between government by a majority and government by a minority. The distinction comes much closer to being one between government by a minority and government by *minorities*. As compared with the political processes of a dictatorship, the characteristics of polyarchy greatly extend the number, size, and diversity of the minorities whose preferences will influence the outcome of governmental decisions. Furthermore, these characteristics evidently have a reciprocal influence on a number of key aspects of politics: the kinds of leaders recruited, the legitimate and illegitimate types of political activity, the range and kinds of policies open to leaders, social processes for information and communication—indeed upon the whole ethos of the society. It is in these and other effects more than in the sovereignty of the majority that we find the values of a democratic process.

V

Our fifth proposition is that in so far as there is any general protection in human society against the deprivation by one group of the freedom desired by another, it is probably not to be found in constitutional forms. It is to be discovered, if at all, in extra-constitutional factors. Take the intensity problem, for example; our brief examination of American constitutional devices for protecting a relatively intense group from deprivation by a larger but relatively more apathetic group came to naught. Yet there may well be protections lying beyond constitutional forms. Without attempting to decide whether relative intensities can really be measured, we can say that if intensities can be measured at all, some kind of overt behavior must be taken as an index. If we accept as an index an individual's own statement about how he feels, then the following important hypothesis seems to be valid:

Political activity is to a significant extent a function of relative intensity.[14]

Now it is also apparent that the probable outcome of a policy decision is partly a function of the relative amount of political activity carried on for or against the alternatives. Hence:

14. For example, as might be expected, voting falls off rapidly from those who are "very much" interested in following a campaign to those who are "not much interested"; or from those who are "very much concerned about the outcome of the election" to those who are "not at all" concerned. Campbell *et al.*, *op. cit.*, Tables 3.6 and 3.8, pp. 35–37. On the other hand, gauged by opinion as to the importance of the outcome to the country, an interesting and unexplained difference is revealed in the sample. Among Eisenhower supporters considerably more of those who felt the outcome made much difference to the country voted than did those who felt the outcome made no difference. Among Stevenson supporters the differences were not statistically significant; actually, in the sample a slightly smaller percentage of those who thought the outcome of much importance to the country voted than among those who thought it of no importance to the country.

All other things being equal, the outcome of a policy decision will be determined by the relative intensity of preference among the members of a group.

The main body of protections, however, is to be found in the preconditions and characteristics of polyarchy; the more fully the social prerequisites of polyarchy exist, the less probable it is that any given minority will have its most valued freedoms curtailed through governmental action. The extent of consensus on the polyarchal norms, social training in the norms, consensus on policy alternatives, and political activity: the extent to which these and other conditions are present determines the viability of a polyarchy itself and provides protections for minorities. The evidence seems to me overwhelming that in the various polyarchies of the contemporary world, the extent to which minorities are bedeviled by means of government action is dependent almost entirely upon non-constitutional factors; indeed, if constitutional factors are not entirely irrelevant, their significance is trivial as compared with the non-constitutional.

VI

What, then, is the significance of constitutional factors?

So far I have avoided a definition of "constitutional." As every political scientist knows, to specify the meaning of "constitutional" at all rigorously is difficult indeed. One is likely to start with a definition and end with a Weltanschauung. Although I do not place much confidence in the utility of my definition, by "constitutional" I propose to mean determinants of governmental decisions (I leave these terms undefined) consisting of prescribed rules influencing the legitimate distribution, types, and methods of control among government officials. The rules may be prescribed by a variety of authorities accepted as legitimate among officials: the written Constitution, if there is one; decisions of a tribunal accepted as authoritative on constitutional interpretation; respected commentaries and the like. By non-constitutional factors, therefore, I mean all other determinants of governmental decisions.

In this sense, all contemporary polyarchies seem to possess such strikingly similar constitutions that the range of the constitutional variable is even more limited than might be thought at first glance. There are two causes for this similarity. In the first place, the characteristics and prerequisites of polyarchy impose a definite limitation on constitutional types available to any large polyarchal society. In the second place, given these characteristics and prerequisites, the efficiencies arising from division of labor impose an additional and highly significant limitation. There is need for a more or less representative body to legitimize basic decisions by some process of assent—however ritualized. Unless the process is entirely ritual, there is within this legislature at least some need for leaders, for committees, and for partisan organizations. There is a need for bureaucracies of permanent experts to formulate alternatives and to make most of the staggering number of decisions that a modern government must somehow make. These bureaucracies must be highly specialized among themselves since they perform highly differentiated tasks: they compete and conflict with one another and with other official groups in the system. Bureaucratic officials must, among other things, make decisions bearing directly upon the actions of particular individuals. Hence a specialized bureaucracy is necessary to pass upon appeals from these preliminary decisions; another specialized bureaucratic task is to adjudicate conflicts among individuals; both tasks are sometimes combined in the same specialized bureaucracy, namely, the judiciary. Bureaucratic, judicial, and legislative decisions must somehow be co-ordinated, and hence a specialized group of officials is needed as co-ordinators. Because the task of co-ordination is so often crucial, involving basic decisions among policy alternatives, it requires leaders of great status and power who can compete successfully at election time. The election process itself requires additional specialization; individuals dedicated mainly to the task of winning elections run nationwide party organizations.

In time, all these manifold specialized groups become vested interests with leaders and non-leaders dependent upon the permanence, the income, the prestige, and the legitimacy of their organizations. They become part of the fundamental warp and woof of the society. In this sense, every polyarchal political system is marked by separation of powers: it has legislature, executive, administrative bureaucracy and judiciary, each of which is, in turn, divided and subdivided; in this sense, too, every polyarchal political system is a system of checks and balances, with numerous groups of officials in competition and conflict with one another.

Given these limits on the range of the constitutional variable, what is the significance of constitutional rules in the operation of democratic politics? So far we have shown that constitutional rules are not crucial, independent factors in maintaining democracy; rather, the rules themselves seem to be functions of underlying non-constitutional factors. We have also shown that the constitutional rules are not significant as guarantors either of government by majorities or of the liberty from majority tyranny.

Our sixth proposition is this: Constitutional rules are mainly significant because they help to determine what particular groups are to be given advantages or handicaps in the political struggle. In no society do people ever enter a political contest equally; the effect of the constitutional rules is to preserve, add to, or subtract from the advantages and handicaps with which they start the race. Hence, however trivial the accomplishments of the constitutional rules may be when measured against the limitless aspirations of traditional democratic thought, they are crucial to the status and power of the particular groups who gain or suffer by their operation. And for this reason, among others, the rules have often been the cause of bitter and even fratricidal struggle.

VII

Viewed in this perspective, we can see the American political system in the light of its special characteristics. Here we come to the seventh and last of the propositions bearing upon the problem of majority tyranny. A central guiding thread of American constitutional development has been the evolution of a political system in which all the active and legitimate groups in the population can make themselves heard at some crucial stage in the process of decision. The remainder of this chapter will be devoted to sketching out in broad strokes the development and character of this system, which I shall refer to as the "normal" American political process.

However, before turning to the way in which this normal system developed, it may be wise to specify what is meant by "active and legitimate." From all that has gone before, it is clear that the politically inactive members of a polyarchal organization cannot directly influence the outcome of decisions.[15] Hence if a group is inactive, whether by free choice, violence, intimidation, or law, the normal American system does not necessarily provide it with a checkpoint anywhere in the process. By "legitimate," I mean those whose activity is accepted as right and proper by a preponderant portion of the active. In the South, Negroes were not until recently an active group. Evidently, Communists are not now a legitimate group. As compared with what one would expect from the normal system, Negroes were relatively defenseless in the past, just as the Communists are now.

A group excluded from the normal political arena by prohibitions against normal activity may nevertheless often gain entry. It may do so (1) by engaging or threatening to engage in "abnormal" political activity—violence, for example; (2) by threatening to deprive groups already within the arena of their legitimacy; or (3) by acquiring legitimacy, and hence motivating the in-groups to incorporate the outgroup. The extension of voting privileges in the period from the American Revolution to Jackson is an example of all three. The belated protection of the lawful franchise of Negroes by the Supreme Court in the past two decades is an instance of the third method. However, as Negroes become a larger part of the active and legitimate electorate, the normal opportunities of the system become open to them and further protection of the franchise can then depend more and more upon use of checkpoints in the normal system. The full assimila-

15. Two seeming exceptions to this are: (1) If active members include among their own goals the protection or advancement of inactive members; (2) if presently active members expect that presently inactive members may become active in the future. Both are important cases in the real world. The first, however, can properly be called a case of indirect rather than direct influence on the outcome. The second merely requires that in principle the time dimension should somehow be specified. This, however, would become too complex for exposition and it is perhaps preferable to let our oversimple proposition stand as it is.

tion of Negroes into the normal system already has occurred in many northern states and now seems to be slowly taking place even in the South.

The "normal" system has developed through several stages. Except for Connecticut and Rhode Island, which continued their relatively democratic colonial charters, all of the states formed new written constitutions between 1776 and 1781. A number of factors—of which democratic ideas were only one—shaped these constitutions. In one respect, however, they tended to be similar: "under most of the Revolutionary constitutions, the legislature was truly omnipotent and the executive correspondingly weak."[16] In eight states, the executive was chosen by the legislature, and in one, New Hampshire, the legislature chose a council, which in turn chose a council president; except in three states, the executive was elected for a one-year term; in six southern states, he could not be re-elected; generally he could not prorogue, adjourn, or dissolve the legislature; the power of appointment was for the most part lodged in the legislature; save for two states, the executive had no power to veto legislation; in every state there was an executive council to watch over him, and in ten states this council was elected by the legislature.

Because of the supremacy of the legislature, these state constitutions have sometimes been regarded as a triumph for populistic democracy,[17] But this is very far from the truth. For the flaw in the system was that the legislatures themselves were frequently highly unrepresentative; in many states legislative supremacy meant not so much the dominance of the people as it meant control over policy by the relatively small elites of wealth and status who were able to control one or both branches of the legislature. The rules, that is to say, were rigged in favor of some groups and against others. Generally speaking, they were rigged in favor of the old centers of population on the seaboard and

16. H. G. Webster, "A Comparative Study of the State Constitutions of the American Revolution," *American Academy of Political and Social Science, Annals*, Vol. IX (1897).

17. Cf. J. Allen Smith, *The Spirit of American Government* (New York: Macmillan Co., 1911), chaps. ii and ix.

against new settlers in the western portions of the states; and they were rigged in favor of the wealthy and against the poor.

Thus in Massachusetts, the Revolutionary constitution established the control of the commercial interests over state policy against the power of the farmers; by heavy property qualifications for both office-holding and voting, the wealthy gained power at the expense of the middling groups and the poor; the Senate, in which representation rested upon taxes paid, was a stronghold of the well-to-do; even the lower house was weighted in favor of the eastern mercantile towns. The legislature and the courts, as might be expected, operated in favor of owners of debt and against the debtors. Debt and poverty went too far; rebellion flared up; Daniel Shays became a brief hero to the indebted and forever a symbol of the dangers of mass tyranny to the wellborn and the few; finally, ruthless repression was followed by mild reform. But the basic balance of benefits and handicaps imposed by the constitution remained unchanged.[18]

18. Cf. Oscar and Mary Flug Handlin, *Commonwealth: A Study of the Role of Government in the American Economy: Massachusetts, 1774–1861* (New York: New York University Press, 1947), pp. 26–27, 41, 44, 45, 49–52, and Appendix II, p. 267. In many respects the Massachusetts constitution was atypical, e.g., the governor had an absolute veto. "Although drafted by a convention elected by manhood suffrage, it was not only one of the most aristocratic of the Revolutionary period but also more thoroughly ensured government by the upper classes than the constitution of 1778 rejected by the same electorate." Elisha P. Douglas, *Rebels and Democrats: The Struggle for Equal Political Rights and Majority Rule during the American Revolution* (Chapel Hill: University of North Carolina Press, 1955), p. 211. In South Carolina, as might be expected, the constitution strengthened tidewater against piedmont. *Ibid.*, pp. 43–44. Cf. also Fletcher M. Green, *Constitutional Development in the South Atlantic States, 1776–1860* (Chapel Hill: University of North Carolina Press, 1930). In an unpublished doctoral dissertation, Norman Stamps has shown how the Connecticut constitution, which was the old colonial charter, was highly democratic in appearance and nicely designed to permit tight control by a tight oligarchy. Norman Stamps, "Political Parties in Connecticut, 1789–1819" (unpublished Ph.D. dissertation, Yale University, 1950). In Pennsylvania the pattern was unique. Universal suffrage was virtually a fact by 1790, forty years before it became general throughout the United States. Evidently because of this the balance remained more nearly favorable to the ordinary farmer and artisan than in other states, even after the constitution adopted under the impetus of radical democracy during the Revolution was displaced in 1789. Douglas, *op. cit.*, chaps. xii–xiv; and Louis Hartz, *Economic Policy and Democratic Thought: Pennsylvania, 1776–1860* (Cambridge: Harvard University Press, 1948), pp. 23 ff. In recent years the rise and decline of these state constitutions has lost the attention of political scientists. This is a pity. They provide a mine of information for the study of political

First and last, the men at the Constitutional Convention in Philadelphia were realists; when they blundered it was not from lack of realism but from lack of knowledge. As realists they understood these things about the constitution they were designing: that constitutional rules must inevitably benefit some groups and penalize others; that the rules were therefore highly controversial and subject to bitter conflict; that the rules must operate within the limits set by the prevailing balance of social forces; that they would, in turn, have consequences for the social balance; and that to endure, a constitution would require the assent of more than the fifty-five distinguished gentlemen in Philadelphia but luckily much less than the whole adult population.

The men at the Convention were perhaps as brilliant an assembly as has ever gathered to devise a lasting constitution for a great nation. It is only an index to the pitiful limitations of human knowledge to note that, realistic and gifted as they were, many of their key assumptions proved to be false, and the constitution they created has survived not because of their predictions but in spite of them.

Madisonian theory provided a brilliant and enduring defense—one is tempted to say rationalization—of the rules they set up. We have seen in what respects the Madisonian approach is deficient. More relevant to our present purposes is the extent to which the members of this historic assemblage did not know what they were doing. They thought the popular House would be dynamic, populistic, egalitarian, levelling, and therefore a dangerous center of power that needed restraint; they thought the President would represent the wellborn and the few and that he would use his veto against popular majorities lodged in the House. They were wrong; for the dynamic center of power has proved to be the presidency, and after Jackson the President could claim, and frequently did claim, to be the only representative of a national majority in the whole constitutional system. Meanwhile, the House has scarcely revealed itself as the instrument of those impassioned majorities that the men at the Convention so desperately

---

institutions, and their decline has never been satisfactorily explained. However, for one aspect of the change, consult Leslie Lipson, *The American Governor: From Figurehead to Leader* (Chicago: University of Chicago Press, 1939).

feared. Today the relationship they envisaged is, by and large, reversed. It is the President who is the policy-maker, the creator of legislation, the self-appointed spokesman for the national majority, whereas the power of Congress is more and more that of veto—a veto exercised, as often as not, on behalf of groups whose privileges are threatened by presidential policy.

Whether the men at the Convention anticipated judicial review is an issue that will probably never be settled; but there is not a single word in the records of the Convention or in the "Federalist Papers" to suggest that they foresaw the central role the court would from time to time assume as a policy-maker and legislator in its own right. They did not foresee clearly, if at all, the great organizing function political parties would perform, and the ways in which these instruments would transform the formal constitutional arrangements. The equal representation of states in the Senate, which has done so much to decentralize the parties, the executive, and, indeed, the entire policy-making process, was not a matter of high constitutional principle but a necessary bargain opposed by many of the best minds at the Convention, including Madison himself.

Most of all, however, the men at the Convention misunderstood the dynamics of their own society. They failed to predict correctly the social balance of power that was to prevail even in their own lifetime. They did not really understand that in an agrarian society lacking feudal institutions and possessing an open and expanding frontier, radical democracy was almost certain to become the dominant and conventional view, almost certain to prevail in politics, and almost certain to be conservative about property.

Despite their false predictions, however, the institutions their work helped to create have in large part survived. Three reasons may account for this: First, for a variety of reasons apotheosis of the Constitution began very early and in an astonishingly short time controversy over the basic constitutional framework was all but eliminated; even the constitutional debate preceding our Civil War was ostensibly concerned with the question of the real intentions of the Convention. Second, perhaps in no society have the conditions of polyarchy been so fully present as they were in the United States in the ante-bellum period (save, of course, for the position of Negroes). To assume that this country has remained democratic because of its Constitution seems to me an obvious reversal of the relation; it is much more plausible to suppose that the Constitution has remained because our society is essentially democratic. If the conditions necessary to polyarchy had not existed, no constitution intended to limit the power of leaders would have survived. Perhaps a variety of constitutional forms could easily have been adapted to the changing social balance of power. It is worth emphasizing again that the constitutional system did not work when it finally encountered, in slavery, an issue that temporarily undermined some of the main prerequisites for polyarchy.

In the third place, the Constitution survived only because it was frequently adapted to fit the changing social balance of power. Measured by the society that followed, the Constitution envisaged by the men at the Convention distributed its benefits and handicaps to the wrong groups. Fortunately, when the social balance of power they anticipated proved to be illusory, the constitutional system was altered to confer benefits and handicaps more in harmony with the social balance of power.

We see this strikingly both in the Jacksonian and in the Congressional phases of development. Had the state constitutions of the Revolutionary period conferred more benefits on the small farmers and artisans and fewer on commerce and tidewater, it is at least possible that when the almost inevitable spread of universal manhood suffrage gave representatives of the small farmers and artisans more control, they would have adapted the national constitutional system in a way quite different from the one which, in fact, they selected. Historical accident also helped to turn agrarian democracy away from legislative supremacy. In highly unified party government led by the President, Jefferson had invented a device that might just barely have permitted the myth of legislative supremacy to survive along with vigorous executive leadership. But Jefferson's system required control by the Congressional caucus over both nominations and policy, and leadership of the caucus by the President. After Jefferson, the caucus seems to have slipped gradually out of the orbit of presidential leadership. By 1824 the forces rallying behind Jackson were unable to make use of it and his election in 1828 spelled the end of the Jeffersonian system.

More than that, Jackson's presidency marks the effective end in this country of the classic identification of democratic rules with legislative supremacy. Radical democrats had feared executive power. Conservative interests in the states favored legislative supremacy because they could control the legislature. Their spokesmen at the Constitutional Convention had in turn feared a national legislature they could not be certain of controlling and looked for their own defense to an executive with veto powers. By working hand in glove with the Congressional caucus, Jefferson overcame the barrier between executive and legislature. Jackson, however, developed a new pattern of relationships, a new constitutional system, and since his day that system has largely prevailed, rather than the Jeffersonian, the Madisonian, or the Revolutionary. The Jacksonian system may be interpreted as asserting that:[19]

1. Groups not effectively represented in the legislature or judiciary may be effectively represented by the executive.

2. The election process confers at least as much legitimacy on the executive's representativeness as on that of the legislature.

3. The President has perhaps a better claim to represent a national majority.

It is the growth of the third principle that, I believe, sets off the period after Jackson from that preceding it, for the idea that the elected executive might be the true representative of the majority was revolutionary in import.

In the post-bellum period, Congress reasserted itself. It would be more accurate to say that highly powerful social groups, driving and ambitious, possessed of rising wealth and status, asserted themselves through Congress. But the power of the new commercial and industrial interests was by no means unlimited; the two political parties were inevitably a hodgepodge of delicate compromises: anything like a comprehensive and co-ordinated national policy was, as the fate of the

19. For example, see W. E. Binkley, *President and Congress* (New York: A. A. Knopf, Inc., 1947), chaps. iv and v.

radical Republicans revealed, impossible. Compromise was maintained, therefore, by a highly decentralized policy-making system that worked essentially by bargaining. Effective control of the political parties was decentralized to state and local machines; control in Congress was decentralized to the committees; and the executive was so decentralized that the President was harldy more than a member of the board of directors of a holding company.

The subsequent growth of bureaucratic organizations under the nominal control of the President or of President and Congress together has been powerfully shaped by the legacy of Congressional government and the political habits and outlooks it gave rise to. In the context of decentralized bargaining parties and a decentralized bargaining legislature, it was perhaps inevitable that despite the powerful efforts of many Presidents and the somewhat Utopian yearnings of many administrative reformers, the vast apparatus that grew up to administer the affairs of the American welfare state is a decentralized bargaining bureaucracy. This is merely another way of saying that the bureaucracy has become a part of what earlier I called the "normal" American political process.

VIII

I defined the "normal" American political process as one in which there is a high probability that an active and legitimate group in the population can make itself heard effectively at some crucial stage in the process of decision. To be "heard" covers a wide range of activities, and I do not intend to define the word rigorously. Clearly, it does not mean that every group has equal control over the outcome.

In American politics, as in all other societies, control over decisions is unevenly distributed; neither individuals nor groups are political equals. When I say that a group is heard "effectively" I mean more than the simple fact that it makes a noise; I mean that one or more officials are not only ready to listen to the noise, but expect to suffer in some significant way if they do not placate the group, its leaders, or its most vociferous members. To satisfy the group may require one or more of a great variety of actions by the responsive leader: pressure for substantive policies, appointments, graft, respect, expression of the appropriate emotions, or the right combination of reciprocal noises.

Thus the making of governmental decisions is not a majestic march of great majorities united upon certain matters of basic policy. It is the steady appeasement of relatively small groups. Even when these groups add up to a numerical majority at election time it is usually not useful to construe that majority as more than an arithmetic expression. For to an extent that would have pleased Madison enormously, the numerical majority is incapable of undertaking any co-ordinated action, It is the various components of the numerical majority that have the means for action.

As this is familiar ground, let me summarize briefly and dogmatically some well-known aspects of the constitutional rules: the groups they benefit, those they handicap, and the net result. When we examine Congress we find that certain groups are overrepresented, in the sense that they have more representatives (or more representatives at key places) and therefore more control over the outcome of Congressional decisions than they would have if the rules were designed to maximize formal political equality.[20] Equal representation in the Senate has led to overrepresentation of the less densely populated states. In practice this means that farmers and certain other groups—metal mining interests, for example—are overrepresented. State legislatures overrepresent agricultural and small-town areas and hence do not redistrict House seats in accordance with population changes; even the House significantly underrepresents urban populations. The operation of the seniority principle and the power of the committee chairman has led the voters in one-party or modified one-party states to be significantly overrepresented. According to one recent estimate, there are twenty-two such states.[21] Geographically these include the solid South, the border states, upper New England, four midwestern states,

20. "Formal" because whether rules designed to maximize formal political equality would actually maximize political equality more than the present rules is a tough empirical question I wish to avoid.

21. Austin Ranney and Willmoore Kendall, "The American Party Systems," *American Political Science Review*, XLVIII (June, 1954), p. 477.

Oregon, and Pennsylvania. Of these only Pennsylvania is highly urban and industrial. Because of the operation of the single-member district system in the House, on the average, a net shift of 1 per cent of the electorate from one party to the other will result in a net gain of about 2.5 per cent of the House seats for the benefited party; and because of the operation of the two-member district in the Senate, a shift of 1 per cent will result in a net gain for the benefited party of about 3 per cent of the Senate seats. Hence when large heterogeneous groups, like the farmers, shift their party support the legislative effects are likely to be considerably exaggerated. (Cf. Figs. 10 and 11.)

All those politicians and officials concerned with the election or re-election of a President, and hence with the vagaries of the electoral college, must necessarily be responsive to a somewhat different set of groups. Again, the general picture is so well known that I need only enumerate a few points. In general the presidential politicians must be responsive to populous states with large electoral votes; to states that are marginal between the parties, i.e., to the two-party states; to the "key" states, i.e., those both marginal and populous; to key groups in the key states—ethnic, religious, occupational; to relatively large nationwide groups; and to heavily populated urban and industrial areas. A careful examination of these will show, I think, that they are different from, and often have goals that run counter to, the groups that predominate in Congress.

The bureaucracies are much more complex. In varying degrees they must be responsive to both presidential and Congressional politicians. But the presidential and Congressional politicians to whom they must respond are themselves rather a narrow and specialized group. In Congress, typically, it is the chairmen of the House and Senate Appropriations Committees, of the relevant subcommittees, and of the relevant substantive committees. Among presidential politicians, administrators must usually be responsive to the Budget Bureau, to the departmental secretary, and, of course, to the President himself. They must also be responsive to their own specialized clienteles. The most effective clientele obviously is one like the farmers, that is also well represented in Congress and even in the executive branch; sometimes bureaucracy and clientele become so intertwined that one cannot easily determine who is responsive to whom.

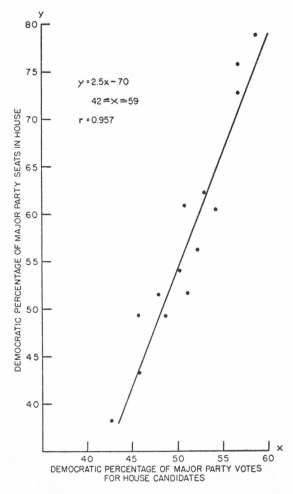

Fig. 10.—Popular votes and Congressional seats won: Democrats in the House of Representatives, 1928–54.

IX

This is the normal system. I have not attempted to determine in these pages whether it is a desirable system of government nor shall I try to do so now. For appraisal of its merits and defects would require

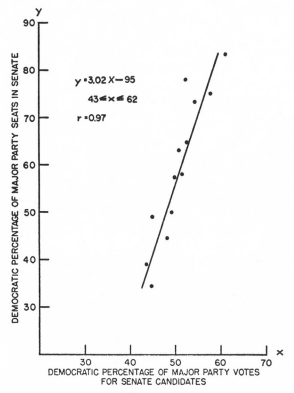

Fig. 11.—Popular votes and Congressional seats won: Democrats in the Senate, 1928–52.

a subtle and extended discussion lying beyond the bounds of these essays.

This much may be said of the system. If it is not the very pinnacle of human achievement, a model for the rest of the world to copy or to modify at its peril, as our nationalistic and politically illiterate glorifiers so tiresomely insist, neither, I think, is it so obviously a defective system as some of its critics suggest.

To be sure, reformers with a tidy sense of order dislike it. Foreign observers, even sympathetic ones, are often astonished and confounded by it. Many Americans are frequently dismayed by its paradoxes; indeed, few Americans who look upon our political process attentively can fail, at times, to feel deep frustration and angry resentment with a system that on the surface has so little order and so much chaos.

For it is a markedly decentralized system. Decisions are made by endless bargaining; perhaps in no other national political system in the world is bargaining so basic a component of the political process. In an age when the efficiencies of hierarchy have been re-emphasized on every continent, no doubt the normal American political system is something of an anomaly, if not, indeed, at times an anachronism. For as a means to highly integrated, consistent decisions in some important areas—foreign policy, for example—it often appears to operate in a creaking fashion verging on total collapse.

Yet we should not be too quick in our appraisal, for where its vices stand out, its virtues are concealed to the hasty eye. Luckily the normal system has the virtues of its vices. With all its defects, it does nonetheless provide a high probability that any active and legitimate group will make itself heard effectively at some stage in the process of decision. This is no mean thing in a political system.

It is not a static system. The normal American system has evolved, and by evolving it has survived. It has evolved and survived from aristocracy to mass democracy, through slavery, civil war, the tentative uneasy reconciliation of North and South, the repression of Negroes and their halting liberation; through two great wars of worldwide scope, mobilization, far-flung military enterprise, and return to hazardous peace; through numerous periods of economic instability and one prolonged depression with mass unemployment, farm "holidays," veterans' marches, tear gas, and even bullets; through two periods of postwar cynicism, demagogic excesses, invasions of traditional liberties, and the groping, awkward, often savage, attempt to cope with problems of subversion, fear, and civil tension.

Probably this strange hybrid, the normal American political system, is not for export to others. But so long as the social prerequisites of democracy are substantially intact in this country, it appears to be a relatively efficient system for reinforcing agreement, encouraging moderation, and maintaining social peace in a restless and immoderate people operating a gigantic, powerful, diversified, and incredibly complex society.

This is no negligible contribution, then, that Americans have made to the arts of government—and to that branch, which of all the arts of politics is the most difficult, the art of democratic government.

Index

Adorno, T. W., 18 n.
Agreement, 78
Amending process, 119
American political system, 137
American Revolution, 138
Aristotle, 34
Arrow, K., 37 n., 42 n., 44
Ashin, M., 6 n.
Autonomy, 79, 80

Barber, B., 72 n.
Bentley, A. F., 131 n.
Berelson, B. R., 77 n., 81 n.
Binkley, W. E., 144 n.
Black, D., 44
Bonham, J., 129 n.
Borda, 43
Brant, I., 13 n.
Bureaucracy, 145, 147
Butler, D. E., 129 n.

Cahill, F., 111 n.
Calhoun, J. C., 29 n., 30 n.
Campbell, A., 72 n., 95, 126 n., 127 n., 134 n.
Canada, 74
Child labor, 106, 109
China, 129 n.
Choate, J., 107
Civil War, 40, 96, 97
Coal miners, 117
Coker, F. W., 37 n.
Commager, H. S., 37 n., 111 n.
Communists, 97, 138

Congress, 55, 59, 105
Connecticut Compromise, 54, 118
Conscience, 18, 36
Consensus, 75, 76, 77, 93, 132
Constitution, 30, 97, 108, 135, 143; checks, 36
Constitutional Convention, 9, 82, 83, 105, 112, 141–42
Cotton, 117
Czechoslovakia, 97

Deadlock, 41
de Grazia, A., 43 n.
de Tocqueville, 35
Dictatorship, 132
Disagreement, 98, 99
Diversity, 78
Douglas, E. P., 10 n., 140 n.
Dred Scott v. Sanford, 109 n.

Eisenhower, D., 95, 96, 126, 126 n.
Elections, 13, 67, 71, 73, 95, 96, 97, 125, 129, 130
Electorate, 105
Elliot's Debates, 7 n., 15 n.
England, 76
Equal representation, 112
Equal rights, 31
Ewing, C. A. M., 111 n.
"External check," 6, 13, 20

Faction, 11, 15, 25, 27, 29
Fair Labor Standards Act, 107
Farm laborers, 115

Farmers, 117
Federalist, The, 5, 6, 9, 10 n., 11 n., 13, 14, 15 n., 20 n., 78
Filibuster, 55
France, 41, 74, 97
Franco, 97
Frank, J. D., 59 n.
Franklin, B., 8
Freedom, 27

Germany, 76
Goldstein, J., 72 n.
Great Britain, 74, 85, 129 n.
Green, F. M., 140 n.
Gurin, G., 72 n., 95, 126 n.

Hamilton, A., 7, 8, 11
Handlin, O., 140 n.
Hartz, L., 10 n., 140 n.
House of Representatives, 146

Index of advantage, 114
Indifference, 38, 39
Intensity, 48, 49, 90, 121, 134, 135
Italy, 74

Jackson, A., 125, 138, 141, 144
Janowitz, M., 18 n.
Jefferson, T., 9, 19, 35, 53, 143
Judicial review, 52, 106, 142
Judiciary, 105

Kahn, R. L., 126 n.
Kendall, W., 37 n., 146 n.
Key, V. O., 87, 127 n.

Lane, R., 18 n.
"Last say," 48
Latham, E., 111 n., 131 n.
Lazarsfeld, P. F., 77 n., 81 n.
Legitimacy, 46, 138
Lenin, 32
Lenoir, 8
Lincoln, A., 35, 40
Lindblom, C. E., 37 n.
Lipset, S. M., 72 n.
Lipson, L., 141 n.
Little, I. D. M., 101 n.
Locke, 34
Louis Napoleon, 97

McClosky, H., 37 n.
Machiavelli, 18
McPhee, W. N., 77 n., 81 n.
Madison, James, 3 ff., 34, 45, 53–54, 78, 82, 98–99, 112, 124, 133
Madisonian argument, 32, Appendix
Madisonian axiom, 10
Majority, 7, 24, 25, 26, 27, 28, 29, 36, 55, 61, 65, 92, 107, 108, 112, 131
Majority faction, 16
Majority principle, 37
Majority tyranny, 9
Marvick, D., 18 n.
Mason, 8
Massachusetts, 140
Merrriam, C., 77 n.
Mexico, 74
Migrant workers, 117
Miller, W. E., 72 n., 95, 126 n.
"Minorities rule," 132
Minority, 7, 21, 25, 26, 27, 28, 30, 31, 36, 65, 92, 107, 112, 128, 131, 133
Minority tyranny, 9
Minority veto, 58
Mosca, G., 54

Nansen, E. J., 42 n., 43 n.
Natural right, 6, 7, 11, 23, 26, 45
Negro rights, 120
Negroes, 59, 115, 117, 138
"Normal" American political process, 138, 145
"Normal" system, 139
Notes on Virginia, 9
Nullification, 28 n.

Oligarchy, 58

Padover, S. K., 6 n., 9 n., 12 n., 29 n.
Participation, 71
Plato, 32, 77 n.
Political activity, 81, 87
Political competition, 132
Political equality, 32, 37, 40, 45, 50, 52, 55, 56
Political parties, 52
Polyarchal democracy, 63 ff.; definition of, 84; measurement of, 85 ff.
Popular sovereignty, 37, 40, 45, 50, 52, 55, 56

Populistic democracy, 38 ff.
Power, 12, 13, 31
Preferences, 66
Presidency, 55, 105, 108, 125, 141, 144
Public opinion, 57

Qualified Minority Rule, 50

Ranney, A., 37 n., 146 n.
Republic, 10
Republican principle, the, 27
Roper, E., 72 n., 131 n.
Rossiter, C., 7 n., 19 n.
Rousseau, 35
Rule, The, 37, 38, 39, 40, 42, 53, 57, 64, 66, 68, 71, 103, 124

Sabine, G. H., 37 n.
Schumpeter, J. A., 131 n.
Secession, 97
Senate, 54, 55, 105, 112, 113, 116, 140, 146
Sharecroppers, 117
Shays, D., 140
Shils, E., 34 n.
Silver, 117
Simon, H., 103 n.
Slavery, 97
Smith, J. Allen, 139 n.
Social checks, 36
Social training, 77, 78
Socrates, 82
South Africa, 74
Spain, 97

Stability, 92, 102
Stamps, N., 140 n.
Starosolskyz, W., 36
Stevenson, A., 95, 96, 126, 129
Stouffer, S. A., 102 n.
Supreme Court, 55, 58, 59, 106, 107, 108, 109, 110, 138
Supreme Court Justices, 110
Swisher, C. B., 107 n.

Transitivity, 42 n.
Truman, D., 131 n.
Truman, H., 126 n., 129
Tyranny, 6, 12, 15, 17, 19, 20, 21, 22, 23, 25, 27, 99, 124, 133

United Nations, 131
United Nations Security Council, 24
United States v. *Lovett*, 59 n.

Veto, 55, 104
Voting, 43, 44, 92

Wage earners, 117
Webb, S. and B., 67 n.
Weber, E. A., 77 n.
Webster, H. G., 139 n.
Wetbacks, 115
Whisky Rebellion, 97
Wilson, F., 87
Woodward, C. V., 121
Woodward, J. L., 72 n.
Wool shorn, 117
Workmen's compensation, 110